3.95

# GOING PLACES WITH GOD

## STEPHEN F. OLFORD

This book is designed for your personal reading pleasure and profit. It is also designed for group study. A leader's guide with helps and hints for teachers and visual aids (Victor Multiuse Transparency Masters) is available from your local bookstore or from the publisher.

**VICTOR BOOKS** a division of SP Publications, Inc.
WHEATON, ILLINOIS 60187

*Offices also in*
Whitby, Ontario, Canada
Amersham-on-the-Hill, Bucks, England

LINCOLN CHRISTIAN COLLEGE

D0291800

All Scripture quotations are from *The New King James Version,* © 1979, 1980, 1982 by Thomas Nelson, Inc., Publishers. Used by permission.

Recommended Dewey Decimal Classification: 248.4
Suggested Subject Heading: CHRISTIAN LIFE

Library of Congress Catalog Card Number: 83-60815
ISBN: 0-88207-320-6

© 1983 by SP Publications, Inc. All rights reserved
Printed in the United States of America

VICTOR BOOKS
A division of SP Publications, Inc.
Wheaton, Illinois 60187

# CONTENTS

69910

# Foreword

Stephen Olford knows the Lord, he knows the Bible, he understands people, and he's been over the road; all of which qualifies him preeminently to write on the pilgrimage of the Christ-follower. In addition, Dr. Olford is one of the most effective communicators I know. When he speaks or writes, it is almost as though he is engraving his words on mind and heart, so carefully, so precisely, does he select his language and order his argument. Lessons he gave two decades ago are still etched on my mind. Once you have heard him, it is easy to quote him verbatim.

What better guide to one's walk with God than that of the "cloud of witnesses" who preceded us. In this book, the ancient people of God pass on to us lessons learned in their walks with God. Inasmuch as our Lord is "the same yesterday, today, and forever," we can live in the confidence that He leads today as He led his ancient people. It may not be a pillar of cloud by day and a pillar of fire by night, but His guidance is no less certain, no less direct, no less dependable. Indeed, whereas His guidance then was from without; now it is from within. Then, there were outward signs; now, He thinks through our minds and moves within our hearts.

The historical record of God's ways with the human family, despite all its weakness, willfulness, and caprice, is strong confirmation of His faithfulness to lead us on our way today despite human frailty.

In this volume Dr. Olford records excellent models which will encourage, inspire, and ennoble those who read. Here is chart and compass for the way, leading through all life's detours, inerrantly to the gate of the city of God.

RICHARD C. HALVERSON, CHAPLAIN
UNITED STATES SENATE

# Introduction

The general theme of this series of studies is *Going Places with God*. I have chosen the title carefully, because I have discovered that God's dealings with His people are specific and definite when it comes to space, time, and sense. Our faith is historic; it has to do with people, places, and purposes in the divine economy.

While this is true throughout the Bible, I have designated the early chapters of Scripture for consideration because of a sequence of truth and thrust we are to follow throughout this study. (In each instance, quotations are from the *New King James Version* of the Bible.)

God is ever leading His people from bondage to blessing, from slavery to victory. In the passages we shall be considering, we shall see this principle unfold.

I invite you to join me in *Going Places with God.*

# Acknowledgments

In sending forth this book to the wider Christian community, I want to make some grateful acknowledgments:

To my many friends and associates who have encouraged me to write a biblically based book on growing and going with God;

To Miss Victoria Kuhl for typing the original notes;

To Rev. Ted S. Rendall, vice-president of Biblical Ministries, Prairie Bible Institute, Alberta, Canada, who invested hours of precious time to research resource materials and appropriate illustrations;

To my dear friend, Dr. Richard C. Halverson, for his sensitive and insightful "Foreword";

To Mrs. Ann Bradley, Director of Communications at Encounter Ministries, for editing and enriching the completed work;

To Heather, my beloved wife, whose companionship and inspiration have made going places with God an exciting experience.

STEPHEN F. OLFORD

7

*To Heather*

# Exodus 14:1-2, 13-15, 19-22, 27, 31; 15:11, 17

Now the Lord spoke to Moses, saying: "Speak to the Children of Israel, that they turn and camp before Pi Hahiroth, between Migdol and the sea, opposite Baal Zephon; you shall camp before it by the sea."

And Moses said to the people, "Do not be afraid. Stand still, and see the salvation of the Lord, which He will accomplish for you today. For the Egyptians whom you see today, you shall see again no more forever. The Lord will fight for you, and you shall hold your peace."

And the Lord said to Moses, "Why do you cry to Me? Tell the Children of Israel to go forward."

And the angel of God, who went before the camp of Israel, moved and went behind them; and the pillar of cloud went from before them and stood behind them. So it came between the camp of the Egyptians and the camp of Israel. Thus it was a cloud and darkness to the one, and it gave light by night to the other, so that the one did not come near the other all that night.

Then Moses stretched out his hand over the sea; and the Lord caused the sea to go back by a strong east wind all that night, and made the sea into dry land, and the waters were divided. So the Children of Israel went into the midst of the sea on the dry ground, and the waters were a wall to them on their right hand and on their left.

And Moses stretched out his hand over the sea; and when the morning appeared, the sea returned to its full depth, while the Egyptians were fleeing into it. So the Lord overthrew the Egyptians in the midst of the sea.

Thus Israel saw the great work which the Lord had done in Egypt; so the people feared the Lord, and believed the Lord and His servant Moses.

"Who *is* like You, O Lord, among the gods? You will bring them in and plant them in the mountain of Your inheritance, in the place, O Lord, which You have made for Your own dwelling."

# 1
## THE PLACE OF
# STARTING

The Children of Israel had been saved from judgment by the shedding and sprinkling of the blood of the lamb. Their march to Canaan had already begun, but in the ordering of God, they were halted by what appeared to be an impossible situation. God Himself had marked out their position "between Migdol and the sea, opposite Baal Zephon" (Ex. 14:2). The sea was before them, Pharaoh's sword behind them, and the mountains around them. In such a situation, the divine command was: *Go forward!*

If you have been to Calvary and experienced the pardon that Jesus gives through His shed and sprinkled blood and are on your way to heaven, there is nothing that need hinder you from going forward with God. The world, the flesh, and the devil have no power against Christians who are prepared to experience a progressive relationship with God.

## A Personal Reliance on God
Such progression must begin somewhere. That starting place is reliance on God. "And Moses said unto the people, 'Do not

be afraid. Stand still, and see the salvation of the Lord. . . . The Lord will fight for you, and you shall hold your peace'" (vv. 13-14). Progress in the Christian life demands a reliance freely reposed in God. "Do not be afraid," Moses said. The Word of God tells us that "the fear of man brings a snare" (Prov. 29:25). When we fear what man can do to us, we become intimidated and entrapped. Such fear is a fundamental betrayal of our love for God, for John reminds us that "perfect love casts out fear" (1 John 4:18).

Reliance is born of a wholehearted love for God. If something or someone is taking the place that God should have in our affections, we will fear in time of crisis. But we have nothing to fear when we trust fully in God.

Freedom from fear is exemplified in the story of a group of scientists and botanists exploring certain almost inaccessible regions of the Alps in search of new species of flowers. One day they spied through binoculars a rare and beautiful flower. It lay in a deep ravine with perpendicular cliffs on both sides. To obtain this rare plant, someone would have to be lowered over the sheer precipice by a rope. Approaching a boy nearby who was watching them with curiosity, they said, "We'll give you five dollars if you'll let us lower you down into the valley below to pick that lovely flower for us."

The youngster, taking a long look down into the dizzy depths, replied, "Just a minute—I'll be right back." When he returned, he was accompanied by an older man. Approaching one of the botanists, the boy said, "I'll go over the cliff and get that flower for you if this man holds the rope. He's my father!"[1]

We must be like this trusting boy. Our spiritual progress demands complete trust in God. "Stand still," cried Moses (Ex. 14:13). A better translation is, "Stand firm." In other words, if you really love God, do not doubt Him—trust Him! If such trust is intelligent and utterly reposed in God, nothing in this world will shake you.

To illustrate this point, Ted Rendall describes a marine creature called a limpet. It lives in a conical shell and clings tenaciously to rocks or timbers at the seashore. It is so sensitive to the approach of danger that when a person comes near, it adheres tightly to its rock. It is almost impossible to pry it loose. The committed Christian should be like a limpet and cling to God no matter what may happen.

How beautifully this is pictured in the life of Job. He had lost everything and then even his own life was threatened, but he stood firm. The testimony that rings out from that furnace of affliction is, "Though He slay me, yet will I trust Him" (Job 13:15).

Moses said, "'See the salvation of the Lord. . . . The Lord will fight for you, and you shall hold your peace'" (Ex. 14:13-14). Relying on God means not only loving God and trusting Him, it means proving Him—allowing Him to do His own special work in our hearts and lives. Paul described this fullness of faith by saying that we "Rejoice in Christ Jesus, and have no confidence in the flesh" (Phil. 3:3). There is much more truth than is sometimes imagined in that often misused expression, *Let go and let God.* When it denotes the full reliance on God to do in and for us what we cannot achieve within ourselves, then it is sound theology.

Harold St. John, in one of his apt illustrations, tells of a group of American ladies who called themselves "The Society of the Queen's Daughters." They decided to make a trip to the Holy Land, and crossed by ship to Palestine. Immediately, they realized their need of a guide, so they hired a man who knew the country well. Before undertaking to guide them around the country and show them the points of interest, he laid down four conditions to which the ladies readily agreed. They were to entrust all their luggage to him, always allow him to go before them, never to act on their own initiative, and to have absolute and implicit confidence in him to make all necessary arrangements in advance for their travel and comfort.

The ladies accepted the terms, but failed to keep the conditions. With regard to the first condition, they were willing to leave the larger, bulkier trunks and suitcases in their guide's charge, but they wanted to hold on to the smaller cases; at his insistence, they handed these over also. When it came time to change trains at an important junction, the ladies, seeing a train on the opposite platform, rushed across and settled themselves comfortably in corner seats without waiting for their guide.

Calmly, their guide took charge: "I'm sorry, ladies, but this train is not going anywhere. Did you not agree to let me go before you and guide you?" Quickly they followed the guide to another platform where their train was waiting.

Later, they had to ride on camels along the edge of a desert to the south of Damascus, and their guide informed them that they would have to spend a night in the desert. Immediately they began to worry: Would there be sleeping facilities? What about food? Would they be safe? But at nightfall they reached an oasis and found that their guide had made every arrangement for their comfort.[2]

So it is with Christians and our guide to heaven, and "they who trust Him wholly find Him wholly true."

In order to clarify what faith involves, C. H. Spurgeon once used this example: Suppose there is a fire on the third floor of a house, and a child is trapped in a room there. A huge, strong man stands on the ground beneath the window where the child's face appears, and calls, "Jump! Drop into my arms!"

It is part of faith to know that there is a man there, still another part of faith to believe him to be a strong man, but the essence of faith lies in trusting him fully and dropping into his arms.[3] The faith that rests fully in God is the faith that involves all three factors—knowledge, trust, and persuasion.

So many people have the notion that once they have received the Saviour's pardon, they are qualified to perfect their salvation through their own energies. This is just what Paul scathingly attacked in his letter to the Galatians: "O foolish Galatians! Who has bewitched you that you should not obey the truth? . . . Having begun in the Spirit, are you now being made perfect by the flesh?" (Gal. 3:1, 3) We gain nothing by our restless and anxious self-efforts.

Many people can identify with Larry Poland who writes: "How I wish I had discovered the Spirit-controlled life years before I did. For 18 years I struggled to produce a kingdom lifestyle on my own. I sought to produce supernatural fruit on my vine through obedience or faithfulness or sincerity." Openly expressing his own failings, he continues: "I tried to live like Jesus without the control of the Spirit of Jesus. My witness was ineffective (five people trusting Christ through it in 18 years). My fruit, when you examined it closely, said 'made in occupied Poland.' My life was a giant roller coaster speeding through slump after slump to 'rededications' of my life to Christ. An extended exercise in frustration. A child of the kingdom living like a faithful member of the Christian world religion. Born to fly and hopping on the ground."[4]

Similarly, the Children of Israel could do nothing to dry up the Red Sea, level the mountains, or annihilate the hosts of Egypt. They had to *let go and let God.* The word to them was, "Stand still, and see the salvation of the Lord . . . . The Lord will fight for you, and you shall hold your peace" (Ex. 14:13-14).

The most subtle characteristic of the self-life is the insistent attempt to do God's work for Him. We think that God is slow, and in our impatience we lash out in self-effort, thus paralyzing progress. God's principle of progress is, "Stand firm, and see."

In other words, *do not panic* but continue loving God, trusting God, and proving God—however seemingly impossible the situation. This is true reliance on God. Only when we whole-heartedly rely on God will He show us the next step.

## A Practical Obedience to God

Going places with God necessitates a personal reliance on God, but of equal importance is a practical obedience to God. "And the Lord said to Moses, 'Why do you cry to Me? Tell the Children of Israel to go forward'" (Ex. 14:15).

This obedience had to be decisive. *Go forward* was a command. This was no time for floundering in a sea of indecision. In retrospect, Lowell's verse applies:

> Once to every man and nation,
> Comes the moment to decide;
> In the strife of Truth with Falsehood
> For the good or evil side.[5]

To go forward was the call of duty, and that was sufficient. The way did not look easy, but that could be no reason for indecision. *Go forward* was the command, and that was enough.

History records the price of decisiveness. W. H. Prescott writes, "Drawing his sword, Pizarro traced a line with it on the sand from east to west. Then, turning south: 'Friends and comrades,' he said, 'on that side are toil, hunger, nakedness, the drenching storm, desertion, and death; on this side, ease and pleasure. There lies Peru with its riches; here, Panama and its poverty. Choose, each man, what best becomes a brave Castilian. For my part, I go to the south.'

"So saying he stepped across the line. He was followed by the brave pilot Ruiz; next by Pedro de Candia, a cavalier, born, as his name imports, in one of the isles of Greece. Eleven others successively crossed the line, thus intimating their willingness to abide the fortunes of their leader, for good or for evil.

"Fame, to quote the enthusiastic language of an ancient chronicler, has commemorated the names of this little band, 'who thus, in the face of difficulties unexampled in history, with death rather than riches for their reward, preferred it all to abandoning their honour, and stood firm by their leader as an example of loyalty to future ages.'"[6]

This obedience had to be God's directive. "And Moses stretched out his hand over the sea . . . and the waters were divided" (Ex. 14:21). How often had these Children of Israel watched that rod of Moses' doing wonders in Egypt? To them it was the symbol of divine authority, power, and discipline. There was no meeting of the board; a committee did not meet in executive session; there was no grappling with the implications of the decision—where the rod pointed, they had to go.

Is anything less required of us today? Do we have access to a directing rod? The answer is crystallized in a little book called A Blade of Grass. "Each one of us is sent of God . . . sent into our surroundings, circumstances, work, temptations, and problems. To be left to wander in them alone would be disaster. But far from wandering alone, aimlessly, we are to have an aim, a direction, a frame through which to view and clarify life's occurrences. The clarifying process is a simple test. Does this fit into the picture God has showed me to be His best for me?"[7] Through His Word and the constant, abiding power of the indwelling Spirit, we need not wander aimlessly—without purpose. The person who obeys the directing rod of divine authority will always find the path of progress. Jesus said, "He who follows Me shall not walk in darkness, but have the light of life" (John 8:12).

Solomon declares, "But the path of the just [the obedient man] is like the shining sun that shines ever brighter unto the perfect day" (Prov. 4:18). The directing rod is the reason Paul could affirm, "For we are His workmanship, created in Christ Jesus for good works, which God prepared beforehand that we should walk in them" (Eph. 2:10). It is why Eliezer could testify, "As for me, being on the way, the Lord led me" (Gen. 24:27). No one can move forward with God without a genuine sense of direction and purpose. Such a guided way is a guarded way: "The pillar of cloud . . . stood behind them" and "the waters were a wall to them on their right hand and on their left" (Ex. 14:19, 22).

This obedience to God had to be divisive. "And Moses stretched out his hand over the sea; and when the morning appeared the sea returned to its full depth" (v. 27). To move forward with God is to put a great divide between the old life and the new. Egypt was now separated from the Children of Israel by a sea of death and destruction. "So the Lord saved Israel that day out of the hand of the Egyptians, and Israel saw the Egyptians dead on the seashore" (v. 30).

Is your obedience to God divisive? Does it separate you from all that God has condemned? Does it cause you increasingly to fear God's judgments against sin on the one hand, and to believe God's goodness to His people on the other? If not, then you are not going forward.

D. L. Moody told a story about two men who, under the influence of liquor, found their way to the dock where their boat was tied. The two men wanted to return home so they got in the boat and began to row. Though they rowed hard all night, they did not reach the other side of the bay. When the gray dawn of the morning broke, they were in exactly the same spot from which they started. They had neglected to loosen the mooring-line and raise the anchor! Mr. Moody used this story as an analogy of the way in which many people are striving to enter the kingdom of heaven. They cannot believe because they are tied to this world. "Cut the cord! Cut the cord!" he would admonish. "Set yourself free from the clogging weight of earthly things, and you will be headed toward heaven."[8]

Obedience to God involves not only a daily willingness and discipline, but a separation from all that God has put under judgment. There is a cause and effect factor at work here; it is only as a result of such obedience that believers can move forward with God.

## A Purposeful Experience of God

Going forward with God is directly and intimately related to a purposeful experience of God. "Then Moses and the Children of Israel sang this song to the Lord" (Ex. 15:1). There was nothing vague or nebulous about their experience of God. On the contrary, their experience was definite as to God's time. "*Then* Moses . . . sang . . . . " This expressive outburst was related to a point in time. God has so ordained things that all experiences on earth can be dated. One reason for this is that we might be able to measure progress in our lives. We were created to be *people in process.* How unfortunate, how sad, that so many people show their lack of progress by revealing the antiquity of their last definite experience of God.

At the close of a meeting in one of the Welsh valley towns, an elderly man said to me, "My dear brother, a vital experience of Christ, such as you have presented tonight, is hardly possible in these strange days in which we live." Looking directly into his face, I asked, "Do you mean to tell me that *you,* the leading member of this church, question the possibility of knowing a present joy and victory in Christ?"

"No," replied my friend, "I would not question the possibility altogether."

"When did you last have such an experience?" I inquired.

"Oh," exclaimed the man with eyes aglow, "you should have seen me in the 1904 revival!"

Thankfully, our experience of God can be more current than that; it can be day by day, moment by moment.

The experience of the Children of Israel was definite as to God's place. "Pharaoh's chariots and his army He has cast into the sea; His chosen captains also are drowned in the Red Sea" (Ex. 15:4).

Charles H. Stevens makes a vital point: "Born out of this experience—their passing through the Red Sea and watching the destruction of Pharaoh and his army—the Children of Israel burst into a song of praise. True praise is always born of a great experience. Someone has said that praise is like the mist that rises from Niagara. Doubtless much of our singing today carries with it little praise because there is much lack of a great experience. We do not venture far with the Lord. We play it safe. For us, it is the paved highway rather than reckless faith in the wilderness and the glory cloud of His presence."[9]

If you look through the Bible, you will find how experiences are related to places. Read the psalms and see how often David described God in terms of some place, simply because it was there that God met with him in a special way. Here, Moses sings of the Red Sea as the place where the Lord was gloriously triumphant. How many of us can similarly speak of specific meeting places in our experiences of God?

If *time* measures our spiritual history, *places* describe our spiritual geography. Progress is vitally related to the places in which God has met with us . . . a quiet hour by a mountain stream; a brisk walk at sunrise; crawling along a ribbon of highway bumper-to-bumper with irate motorists. Places may indicate a straight line along God's will or a zigzag trail of shameful backsliding. Whatever the situation, places are definite markers of our progress.

There can be no question that the experience of the Children of Israel was definite as to God's aim. One cannot study this song without observing a threefold aim of a purposeful experience of God. First, there is a new experience of wonder. "Who is like You, O Lord, among the gods? Who is like You, glorious in holiness, fearful in praises, doing wonders?" (v. 11) The mark of spiritual health and progress is the increasing sense of wonder which comes through the contemplation of God's Person and work. Any form of irreverent familiarity in holy things is the evidence of stagnation and backsliding. God have mercy on us if and when things of the Spirit fail to fill our souls with wonder!

Second, there is a new experience of worship. "Then Moses and the Children of Israel sang this song to the Lord" (v. 1). Where there is genuine wonder, there is true worship. The song was "to the Lord." John Wesley conducted an open-air service in a little village in Cornwall over 200 years ago and wrote: "I preached Christ our 'wisdom, and righteousness, and sanctification.' I could not conclude till it was so dark that we could scarce see one another. And there was on all sides the deepest attention; none speaking, stirring, or scarce looking aside. Surely here, though in a temple not made with hands, was God worshiped in the beauty of holiness."[10]

Our text says that the song was "to the Lord." You do not find a single note about self—its doings, sayings, or feelings. Up to this time, the Children of Israel were full of themselves. If their voice was heard, then it was the cry of sorrow amid the brick kilns of Egypt, or the wail of distress when surrounded by what they deemed to be insuperable difficulties. But then they burst into song; self was completely forgotten in the sheer rapture of lauding the praises of their delivering God. This is spiritual worship: the overflow of joyfulness in the Holy Spirit.

Precisely this attitude was expressed by longtime soloist George Beverly Shea, when he wrote:

> Oh, the wonder of it all! The wonder of it all!
> Just to think that God loves me.[11]

Third, there is a new experience of witness. "The people will hear . . . the chiefs of Edom will be dismayed; the mighty men of Moab (shall tremble) . . . the inhabitants of Canaan will melt away" (vv. 14-15). Where there is true worship, there is powerful witness. God was so real to the Children of Israel just then that they wanted the common people to hear, the exalted people to be amazed, the strong people to tremble, and the hostile people to melt away as a result of their witness.

Are these principles of progress vital in YOUR life? If they are, then continue to go forward—for progress is the law of the Christian life as well as that of the universe.

If these principles of progress are not operative in your life, then seek restoration at once from backsliding and go forward with God. Do not be dissuaded from seeking to become an in-depth Christian. "I know of some pastors in strategic churches," writes James Mahoney, "who have been 'turned off' from much emphasis on the deeper spiritual life. They have seen so many who supposedly have experienced great personal victory, yet do little to share Christ with others."[12]

Be courageous; share your faith and say along with Paul, "Forgetting those things which are behind and reaching forward to those things which are ahead, I press toward the goal for the prize of the upward call of God in Christ Jesus" (Phil. 3:13-14).

If you have never begun to go forward, then begin immediately, lest you be overthrown in the midst of the sea of God's judgments.

What I say to one, I say to all: *Go forward! Go forward with God!*

# Exodus 15:22-27

So Moses brought Israel from the Red Sea; then they went out into the Wilderness of Shur. And they went three days in the wilderness and found no water. Now when they came to Marah, they could not drink the waters of Marah, for they were bitter. Therefore the name of it was called Marah.

And the people murmured against Moses, saying, "What shall we drink?"

So he cried out to the Lord, and the Lord showed him a tree; and when he cast it into the waters, the waters were made sweet. There He made a statute and an ordinance for them. And there He tested them, and said, "If you diligently heed the voice of the Lord your God, and do what is right in His sight, give ear to His commandments and keep all His statutes, I will put none of these diseases on you which I have brought on the Egyptians. For I am the Lord who heals you."

Then they came to Elim, where there were twelve wells of water, and seventy palm trees: so they camped there by the waters.

69910

## 2

THE PLACE OF

# HEALING

The Bible teaches and experience proves that after conversion our next greatest need is for daily cleansing or healing. Our actions and attitudes within the framework of normal living soon reveal that we have natures that require the constant application of God's cleansing and healing power.

In the journey from Egypt to Canaan, the Children of Israel came to a place called Marah, or bitterness. This place was but the reflection of a condition that is to be found in every human heart. It only requires a given set of circumstances, and bitterness—which is really the sin of rebellion and resentment against God—will surface.

## The Problem

For the moment, let's focus on the problem that precipitated healing. "So Moses brought Israel from the Red Sea; then they went out into the Wilderness of Shur. And they went three days in the wilderness and found no water. Now when they came to Marah, they could not drink the waters of Marah, for they were bitter. Therefore the name of it was called Marah" (Ex. 15:22-23).

We should not assume that the Children of Israel came upon this situation by chance. It is evident that the people (2½ million of them, in all probability) were actually following Moses, who in turn, was moving with the pillar of cloud and of fire. In other words, this bitterness lay right in the path of God's leading, direction, and guidance.

Christians often ignore the fact that God, in His overruling providence, allows His people to go through periods of testing. Henry Van Dyke helps us understand the validity of such testing in *The Challenge of Resistance*: "No doubt a world in which matter never got out of place and became dirt, in which iron had no flaws and wood no cracks, in which gardens had no weeds, and food grew already cooked, in which clothes never wore out and washing was as easy as the soapmakers' advertisements describe it, in which rules had no exceptions and things never went wrong, would be a much easier place to live in. But for purposes of training and development it would be worth nothing at all.

"It is the resistance that puts us on our mettle; it is the conquest of the reluctant stuff that educates the worker. I wish you enough difficulties to keep you well and make you strong and skillful!"[1]

We should be thankful for God's refining process. We should not, as Peter says, be doubtful, perplexed, or amazed because of the fiery trials that will try us (1 Peter 4:12), nor should we think of ourselves as being necessarily unfavored by God when we pass through times of temptation.

If we carefully study our Lord's temptation, we find that He faced the world, the flesh, and the devil. Yet, after 40 days of fasting, praying, and reading (Deut. 9:9; 10:10), He was able to say to the devil, "It is written;" "It is written;" "It is written." (See Matt. 4:4, 7, 10.) With that affirmative thrust of the sword of the Word, the devil left Him for a season.

I appreciate the way Alan Redpath tells that story. He depicts our Lord's confrontation with the devil. With sanctified common sense, he portrays the devil looking at the Lord Jesus, and saying: "I can beat You." But the Lord Jesus answers: "As God of very God I could annihilate you with one breath of My mouth, but I'm *not* going to face you as God. I'm going to face you as man." Then Alan Redpath quickly adds: *And He beat him—AS A MAN!*

These Hebrews, having been delivered from the Egyptians, immediately went into the wilderness, and after three days found themselves without water. Because of their evil hearts of unbelief, they became bitter and resentful. This problem arose from dual causes, the first being the failure of human resource. "And they went three days in the wilderness and found no water" (Ex. 15:22).

Of course, here the lack of water represents human inadequacy. When we count on human resource there is always failure and disappointment. This is true especially in the matter of spiritual growth. LeRoy Eims writes, "If you have fallen into the trap of struggling for holiness and purity of life, then realize that it doesn't come that way. It is by surrender, not struggle."[2] If we are going to have water at all, it must be water from heaven. Only then will it be "a fountain of water springing up into everlasting life" (John 4:14).

Remember how God complained through Jeremiah concerning His people? "For My people have committed two evils: they have forsaken Me, the fountain of living waters, and hewn themselves cisterns—broken cisterns that can hold no water" (Jer. 2:13).

Where was the source of the water used by the Children of Israel? Egypt. As they came through the Red Sea with their wagons, they carried those skins, or vessels, full of water, but human resource was soon depleted. When they discovered no water in their vessels, they looked for a river and found one. It must have been a considerable river, because from it at least 2 million people and their cattle eventually drank. The very sight of that river made them feel that all was well. But what they had to learn was that with the failure of human resource there is a second part of the cause of bitterness which is the nature of human recourse.

When the water they carried failed, it appeared, at first, that there was no problem. After all, there was a river ahead of them. Here was their recourse. What they did not know, however, was the nature of human recourse. Scholars tell us that the water was not only bitter, but was contaminated, and therefore capable of transmitting disease. That is why God described Himself, on this occasion, as the *Healer* (Ex. 15:26).

The failure of human resource always reveals the nature of human recourse. The problem points up the failure and nature of your life and mine, apart from the grace of God. Speaking of this in another context, Paul wrote, "In me (that is, in my flesh) nothing good dwells; for to will is present with me, but how to perform what is good I do not find" (Rom. 7:18). That is Marah—bitterness: your problem and mine.

## The Poison

In addition to the problem of bitterness there was something worse. It was the poison that necessitated healing. "And the people murmured against Moses, saying, 'What shall we drink?'" (Ex. 15:24) The commentary of the Holy Spirit on the danger of bitterness is plain and penetrating: "Nor let us tempt Christ . . . nor murmur, as some of them also murmured" (1 Cor. 10:9-10). The acid test as to whether a person is in true victory is simply this: when the challenge comes, does he turn to the Lord with the faith of contentment, or run from the Lord with the fire of resentment?

Francis de Sales has expressed an understanding of the depth of contentment with which we should be concerned: "Do not look forward," he has written, "to the changes and chances of this life in fear; rather look to them with full hope that, as they arise, God, whose you are, will deliver you out of them. He has kept you hitherto . . . and He will lead you safely through all things; and when you cannot stand, He will bear you in His arms . . . . Either He will shield you from suffering, or He will give you unfailing strength to bear it. Be at peace, then, and put aside all anxious thoughts and imaginations."[3]

Where there is resentment and bitterness, there is the poison of destructive criticism. "And the people murmured against Moses" (Ex. 15:24). Moses was the leader commissioned by God to take His people to the Promised Land. He was doing exactly what God had directed him to do: march with the people and follow the cloud, but they murmured against him. He had guided the people to this very point and what had happened? There was no water and Marah was bitter.

While contending with the many problems of geography and climate in the building of the Panama Canal, Colonel George Washington Goethals had to endure the carping criticisms of countless busybodies back home who predicted that he would never complete his great task. But the resolute builder pressed steadily forward in his work and said nothing.

"Aren't you going to answer your critics?" a subordinate inquired.

"In time," Goethals replied.

"How?"

The great engineer smiled. "With the canal," he replied.[4]

Well could Moses, the leader of God's people, have said to his subordinates: "I'll answer my critics in time—with the conquest of Canaan. No problem that lies between us and that goal is too great for God to handle."

When we take our eyes off the Lord during periods of testing, inevitably we begin to blame other people; our perspectives become blurred. Moses was not to be blamed in this instance, but such is the perverseness of human nature that people often do not see beyond the immediate to the ultimate. Under periods of testing, God's people should never make snap judgments, because those judgments are usually, if not always, wrong.

The poison of destructive criticism is always associated with the poison of disruptive cynicism. "What shall we drink?" (Ex. 15:24) There was only one thing they could drink and that was water, but it had to be the water of God's provision. This is where they were disruptively cynical. To be caught up in disruptive cynicism is like being caught in the doldrums. In the days when ocean vessels were driven by wind and sail, nothing was so feared as the doldrums. The doldrums is a part of the ocean near the equator, abounding in calms, squalls, and light, baffling winds. There the weather is hot and extremely dispiriting. The old sailing vessels, when caught in the doldrums, would lie helpless for days and weeks on end, waiting for the wind to blow.[5]

Lethargy, in the spiritual sense, hinders all creative activity, consumes our energy in and of itself, and distorts our perspectives. When we are out of God's will, we not only blame the wrong people, but we ask the wrong questions. Under pressure and with our eyes off the Lord, we blame those people around us and closest to us for our problems. We fail to see our problems as opportunities for God to demonstrate His power. We get ourselves clogged in utter confusion and frustration because there seems to be no answer. But we must learn that God never answers the wrong question; He only answers the right question, even with regard to the prayer of faith.

## The Purging

The problem and poison of bitterness must be matched with the purging that brings healing. "So [Moses] cried out to the Lord, and the Lord showed him a tree; and when he cast it into the waters, the waters were made sweet. There He made a statute and an ordinance for them. And there He tested them" (v. 25).

It is important to understand the symbolism in the Bible to know what that tree represents. Peter writes, "Who Himself bore our sins in His own body on the tree, that we, having died to sins, might live for righteousness—by whose stripes you were healed" (1 Peter 2:24). Paul adds, "Cursed is everyone who hangs on a tree" (Gal. 3:13).

The character of the death of our Lord Jesus Christ is not only redemptive; it is cosmic. There is no situation in which you can find yourself for which Jesus Christ did not die. "So he cried out to the Lord; and the Lord showed him a tree" (Ex. 15:25). With some appropriate instrument, Moses cut the tree and in so doing, he symbolically illustrated what happened when Jesus died upon the cross. When Christ submitted to those nails in His hands and His feet, He was, in fact, "cut off from the land of the living; for the transgressions of My people He was stricken" (Isa. 53:8). That symbolical cut of the tree was the death of the Saviour. Moses took that severed tree and *plunged* it into the water; in other words, he applied the cross to the problem.

Then what happened? When he had cast it into the waters, "the waters were made sweet" (Ex. 15:25). Whatever poison was in that water creating disease was immediately cleansed and the waters became pure and sweet again. There is no bitterness of experience in our lives that cannot be sweetened by the cross of our Lord Jesus Christ. "The blood of Jesus Christ His Son cleanses us from all sin" (1 John 1:7). It makes no difference how deep the problem is, thank God, the Cross is more than adequate.

Having demonstrated that He had an answer to every problem by the wonderful miracle that was performed, God said something to His people. Through Moses came the corrective answer to the people. "There He made a statute and an ordinance for them. And there He tested them and said, 'If you diligently heed the voice of the Lord your God, and do what is right in His sight, give ear to His commandments and keep all His statutes, I will put none of these diseases on you which I have brought on the Egyptians. For I am the Lord who heals you'" (Ex. 15:25-26).

What was God's answer to the people? Initially, they were to hear His voice. The reason they went wrong was because they did not *hear* the Lord's voice. I don't know at what point they missed out, but if they had lifted their hearts to the Lord at that time he would have answered, just as He answered Moses.

Asking God to meet our needs presupposes an active faith in Him. "Faith does not believe in a God who just 'exists,' as I may believe that an equestrian statue exists in a city in South Africa," explains Dr. Sam Shoemaker. "Faith believes in a God who lives, and loves, and reaches out to man, and down to him, helping him with his life, guiding him in the way he reacts to difficulties, strengthening him where he is weak and using him—when he is open—to serve His great divine ends and purposes."[6]

I know nothing that marks a true Christian walk more than listening to God's voice. Jesus said, "My sheep hear My voice, and I know them, and they follow Me" (John 10:27). When standing before Pilate, with the darkness of the Cross before Him, Jesus said, "Everyone who is of the truth hears My voice" (18:37). That statement can be alternately translated, "Everyone who is of reality," or "Everyone that is characterized or distinguished by reality" will hear God's voice. People who follow close to the Lord Jesus Christ will never be tempted to murmur or grumble or complain because they are hearing His voice and that is all that matters.

The next dimension was that they were not only to hear His voice, but they were to seek His face. "Diligently heed the voice of the Lord your God, and do what is right in His sight" (Ex. 15:26). In the Old Testament the sight of God, the eyes of God, are symbolic of walking in the light. That is why the priests used to pronounce the blessing: "The Lord bless you and keep you; the Lord make His face shine upon you, and be gracious to you; the Lord lift up His countenance upon you, and give you peace" (Num. 6:24-26). The shining of the face of Jehovah, the light of His face, was always an evidence of the favor of God, of walking in the light, of communion with God. By the same token, whenever God turned away His face, it was because the people lost favor—they had sinned and were out of the light.

Jesus said, "I am the light of the world. He who follows Me shall not walk in darkness, but have the light of life" (John 8:12). John, undoubtedly remembering that statement, says, "If we walk in the light as He is in the light, we have fellowship with one another, and the blood of Jesus Christ His Son cleanses us from all sin" (1 John 1:7).

You can always tell a man who is hearing the voice of Jesus because he can hear the voice of the Word, the voice of the Spirit, and he can seek the face of Jesus at any moment, in any situation. It is a lifting of the heart, a looking away to heaven in unbroken communion.

With constancy, the Children of Israel were to know His grace. "If you diligently heed the voice of the Lord . . . and do what is right in His sight, give ear to His commandments and keep all His statutes, I will put none of the diseases on you which I have brought on the Egyptians" (Ex. 15:26). That concept of healing, of course, is the unmerited grace of God applied to all our needs. A person walking in obedience knows the grace of his Lord moment by moment, and there is a constant purging and healing each day. David, the shepherd, soldier, and sovereign knew nothing of fragmented grace of God in his life. He could say, "He [Jehovah] restores my soul" (Ps. 23:3). And because of that restoring grace, David had no want in life and no worry in death. He affirms, "The Lord is my shepherd; I shall not want (v. 1), adding, "Though I walk through the valley of the shadow of death, I will fear no evil . . . goodness and mercy shall follow me all the days of my life" (vv. 4, 6).

George Mueller, the founder of the Bristol Orphanage, was relating to a friend some of the difficulties he had to contend with in providing the orphans with food day and night. When he had finished, his friend said to him, "You seem to live from hand to mouth!" "Yes," said Mueller, "but it's my mouth and God's hand."[7]

Even though we are saved and on our way to heaven, that old nature within us still acts and reacts in bitterness and resentment. But thank the Lord, with the problem and poison of bitterness there is purging. God has the answer and we must hear His voice, seek His face, and know His grace if we are to enjoy a life of victory.

# Exodus 15:27

Then they came to Elim, where there were twelve wells of water and seventy palm trees; so they camped there by the waters.

# 3

## THE PLACE OF

# *RESTING*

Archeologists and biblical scholars have long tried to locate Elim. Many believe that it is one of the beautiful fertile valleys between what we know today as Suez and Sinai. Apparently, in the rainy season this valley filled up with water and poured its torrents into the Red Sea.

I want to point out that this was *not* Canaan. Canaan still lay ahead of the Children of Israel. Canaan represents the fullness of the blessing of the Gospel of Christ—the place to which God is bringing all His people who remain faithful to Him. Our God is a gracious God, for even on the way to Canaan He leads us through Marah to teach us the meaning of healing and then through Elim to teach us the meaning of resting; a foretaste of what we are going to have when we get into Canaan.

When the Children of Israel came to Elim they were no longer wandering. They came to Elim by divine appointment, which involved God's direction and protection. They had come through the Red Sea; on the other side, the pillar of fire had appeared before them. Wherever that cloud moved, the camp followed. It was the symbol of God's immediate presence with His people. It was what we call today the leading of the Spirit of God in the life of a believer. "For as many as are led by the Spirit of God, these are the sons of God" (Rom. 8:14).

Sonship was a special privilege accorded those who had reached the age of reason. Having been taught the Law and the customs, they were capable of following the leadership they had been given. When the Holy Spirit brings us to that place of sonship of which Paul speaks in Romans 8, we know that one of the greatest experiences in the Christian life is to be led by the Spirit.

We can learn much from the life of George Mueller: "I never remember in all my Christian course that I ever sincerely and patiently sought to know the will of God by the teaching of the Holy Spirit through the instrumentality of the Word of God, but I have always been rightly directed. But if honesty of heart and uprightness before God were lacking, or if I did not patiently wait on God for instruction, or if I preferred the counsel of my fellowmen to the declarations of the Word of God, I made great mistakes."[1]

It is imperative that we be guided by the Spirit. Unless we know the place of God's appointment in our lives, we will drift aimlessly. We need to *live* Romans 8—we need to live by the power of the enabling Spirit; otherwise we will miss the mark.

## The Restfulness of Security

The restfulness of security not only means the direction of God, it means the protection of God. Think about that word *Elim*. Some scholars interpret it as palm trees; others say that it means oaks. There are still others who maintain that the word means strong, or ram, or stag. Together those definitions convey the thought of shelter, protection, and strength.

When that multitude of people following Moses and the pillar of cloud arrived at Elim, they felt a sense of security as they saw those 70 palm trees standing like a military guard. To follow the Lord Jesus Christ is to know the security of His protection. "Though I walk through the valley of the shadow of death, I will fear no evil; for You are with me; Your rod and Your staff, they comfort me (Ps. 23:4).

During the dark days of World War II, a British liner left an English port, bound for America. The crossing was very dangerous. Secret directions were given to the liner's captain. They read: "Keep straight on this course. Turn aside for nothing, and if you need help, send a wireless message in this code!" After a few days at sea, an enemy cruiser was sighted. The captain's message, decoded, read, "Enemy cruiser sighted. What shall I do?" Back came the reply from an unseen ship: "Keep straight on; I am standing by." Though no friendly vessel could be seen, the liner kept straight on, and at last reached port in safety. Soon afterward, there steamed into the same harbor a British man-of-war. The battleship, though unseen, had been standing by all the time, ready to help in time of need.[2]

God is the protector of His children. In danger, His mighty arms are about us. Though we cannot see Him, we know that He is in the shadows, keeping watch over His own. The way of God's appointment is the place of God's direction and protection.

## The Restfulness of Sufficiency
"Then they came to Elim, where there were twelve wells of water and seventy palm trees (Ex. 15:27). In this verse we see the restfulness of sufficiency. Moses, by the inspiration of the Holy Spirit, recorded the number of wells and palm trees. Devotional expositors down through the centuries have sought to

make much of these numbers, but I think there is a significance which we dare not press too far. The obvious interpretation of these numbers is that of sufficiency. We are assured of the sufficiency of the Spirit for every need.

The well is used both in John 4 and John 7 to set forth two aspects of the Spirit's ministry in the believer's life. First, there is the indwelling of the Spirit. Speaking to the woman of Samaria, the Lord Jesus said, "Whoever drinks of this water will thirst again, but whoever drinks of the water that I shall give him will never thirst. But the water that I shall give him will become in him a fountain of water springing up into everlasting life" (John 4:13-14). *It is a good thing when a person substitutes the bucket for a spring.* If you are genuinely following Christ, you have a divine spring of water in your life. Have you ever tried to suppress a spring? This was one of our pastimes as boys in Central Africa, but the faster we worked, the more that water bubbled out everywhere!

In the Columbia River there is a famous spot where a well springs up at low tide and people dip their buckets or cups in that pure, clear water and drink. Then the tide comes in and that spring is immersed. You are tempted to think that the spring has stopped flowing. But when you dive down, you can see bursting forth from that one spot a spout of clear, pure water. Whether seen or unseen, it goes on bubbling. We can never complain about our circumstances if we have a well springing up into everlasting life.

These wells—12 of them—speak of the ministry of the indwelling Spirit and also of the infilling of the Spirit. This leads us to John 7 where Jesus says, "'He who believes in Me, as the Scripture has said, out of his heart will flow rivers of living water.' But this He spoke concerning the Spirit, whom those believing in Him would receive; for the Holy Spirit was not yet given; because Jesus was not yet glorified" (vv. 38-39). To live the deeper life, we must be convinced of the power of the indwelling Spirit. Everyone who is born again has in him the spring of water. But a person can know the indwelling of the Holy Spirit without knowing the infilling of the Spirit. What makes the difference? If you are born again of the Spirit of God, you have a well of water already in you. But there are many Christians from whose lives the rivers of living water are not flowing. Why is that? John gives us the answer in verse 39. Just as the Holy Spirit was not poured forth in Pentecostal effusion and profusion until Jesus was literally glorified, so, experientially, the Holy Spirit is never poured forth in fullness until Jesus is glorified in the life.

Standing on the deck of a ship in mid-ocean, you can see the sun reflected from its depth. From a little boat on a mountain lake, you can see the sun reflected from its shallow waters. Looking into the mountain spring not more than six inches in diameter, you can see the same great sun. Look into the dewdrop of the morning, and there it is again. The sun has a way of adapting itself to its reflections. The ocean is not too large to hold it, nor the dewdrop too small. So God can fill any man, whether his capacity be like the ocean, like the mountain lake, like the spring, or like the dewdrop. Whatever, therefore, be the capacity, there is the possibility of being filled with the fullness of God.[3]

Twelve springs. Have you thought about that—the glorious sufficiency of it all? The entire year is gathered up. Isn't it interesting that when the Lord Jesus fed the multitude there were 12 baskets taken up? It speaks of the superabundance of the supply of the Holy Spirit, the plentitude of power, grace, and gifts in the Spirit. What a place Elim is!

We would be remiss if we embrace the sufficiency of the Spirit of God for every need but fail to give attention to the sufficiency of the Scriptures for every need. The psalmist tells us that the blessed man is the one who meditates on the Word of God day and night, whose leaf never withers, whose fruit is always plentiful. (See Ps. 1:1-3.) Show me a man who persistently and consistently lives in the Word and I will show you a man who is a tree—evergreen and fruitful.

There are three things about the trees on which I want to focus. First, a tree suggests life. The Saviour made this clear when He said, "The words that I speak to you are spirit, and they are life" (John 6:63). Let's never forget that the written Word of God is a communication of the living Son of God. As I read the Bible, and the Holy Spirit makes it real to me, it is life—life abundant.

W. E. Biederwolf recalls the story of a young artist who had worked long on the statue of an angel. Upon its completion the artist concealed himself to hear what the master Angelo would say about it. When he heard the master say, "It only lacks one thing," the artist became distraught and could neither eat nor sleep until a friend, out of deep concern, went to Angelo's studio inquiring what it was the statue lacked. The great artist said, "Man, it lacks only life! If it had life it would be as perfect as God Himself could make it."[4] When you became a child of God, you became a partaker of life, but it is possible to live on the growing edge. Peter tells us that by appropriating the "exceedingly great and precious promises" we become "partakers of the divine nature" (2 Peter 1:4). The divine nature is nothing less than the life of God—what Jesus called abundant life (John 10:10).

Second, where there is life, there is growth. "As newborn babes, desire the pure milk of the Word, that you may grow thereby" (1 Peter 2:2). This is a principle we sometimes overlook. Every Christian worker has a right to challenge those to whom they minister if there is no growth. Are you growing? You can tell in many ways if there is an evidence of growth.

Just as a child grows out of his clothes; just as a child begins to develop in so many ways—spirit, soul, and body; just as a child becomes deeper in his impressions, wider in his ambitions and desires, so in the Christian life the same is true. *Where there is life, there is growth,* and there is no doubt about the evidences of such development.

Third, where there is life and growth, there will be fruit. Have you ever noticed how the Lord Jesus links the Word of God abiding in us with fruit? Jesus said, "If you abide in Me, and My words abide in you, you will ask what you desire, and it shall be done for you. By this My Father is glorified, that you bear much fruit; so you will be My disciples" (John 15:7-8). The Master has already spoken of fruit, more fruit, but here is much fruit. Here are 70 palm trees. John 15 makes it clear that fruit is always regarded in two ways. It is the fruit of character—Christlikeness, which is "love, joy, peace, long-suffering, kindness, goodness, faithfulness, gentleness, self-control" (Gal. 5:22-23). There is also the fruit of service: "You did not choose Me, but I chose you and appointed you that you should go and bear fruit, and that your fruit should remain" (John 15:16). Is there fruit in our lives? John Bunyan said, "If I were fruitless, it mattered not who commended me; if I were fruitful, I cared not who did condemn." What the Saviour is looking for in our lives is fruit; and if we are living in Elim there is not just one tree, but 70 of them, the abundance of fruit.

## The Restfulness of Serenity

Finally, Elim represents the restfulness of serenity. "They camped there by the waters" (Ex. 15:27). This statement graphically depicts Christian serenity. David expresses the same concept when he says, "The Lord is my shepherd; I shall not want" (Ps. 23:1). What we have is the serenity of being settled. In the psalm to which I have just referred, David goes on to say that when the shepherd leads his sheep into green pastures, he makes them to lie down. There are two reasons why the sheep will lie down in green pastures. The first is that they are satisfied. Hungry sheep will never lie down; they will wander away anywhere and everywhere in search of food. But within the provision of the shepherd the sheep will lie down. The other reason is that in those green pastures there is quietness and restfulness. Intuitively, the sheep know that they are safe while the shepherd stands by with his rod and staff.

Dr. H. W. McLaughlin tells of a lovely experience he had while in Palestine. In talking to an old shepherd he inquired in what sense it could be said that his staff was for the comfort of the sheep. The shepherd explained that in daylight he always carried the staff across his shoulder, and when the sheep saw it, it spoke of the presence of the shepherd. On the other hand, if night overtook him with the sheep on the mountainside, or if they were caught in a heavy mountain mist so that the sheep could no longer see the staff, then he would lower it. As he walked he would tap with it on the ground so that by hearing if not by sight the staff comforted the sheep by speaking of the presence of the shepherd.[5]

When the Children of Israel reached Elim, it became the place of resting; they enjoyed the serenity of being settled. There is nothing more precious in the Christian life than experiencing peace with God: it is enjoying the peace of God. The Apostle Paul refers to this when he says, "The peace of God, which surpasses all understanding, will guard your hearts and minds through Christ Jesus" (Phil. 4:7).

Implicit in this restfulness of serenity is the serenity of being strengthened. Notice that the Children of Israel camped by the waters. The Psalmist David led his sheep not only into the pastures of tender grass, but by the waters of stillness. These waters have always been interpreted as symbolic of the strengthening power of the Holy Spirit. There is nothing more weakening and debilitating than a dehydrated body. But in the thoughtful provision of the shepherd, there are always wells of water.

At Elim there were 12 wells. This reminds me of that phrase in Paul's letter to the Ephesians, where he speaks of "the exceeding greatness of His power toward us who believe" (Eph. 1:19). No wonder he could pray for those believers at Ephesus that they might be "strengthened with might through His Spirit in the inner man" (3:16). Only by such strengthening can we know the fullness and freshness of the Saviour's indwelling. Apart from the empowering Spirit, the Christian is completely helpless. "In me (that is, in my flesh) nothing good dwells" (Rom. 7:18). This is what Jesus meant when He declared, "Without Me you can do nothing" (John 15:5). How wonderful to know that by the power of His enabling Spirit we can do all things.

Two men were visiting a factory. They were being shown the rooms where huge machines were operating; inside those rooms the noise level was extremely high. Then the guide showed the men a smaller room. It was very quiet. One of the men commented that there was not much going on in that particular room. But the guide replied, "This is the most important room in the entire plant. This is where the power comes from to run the huge machines. We call this room 'The Quiet Room.'" The visitors looked with new respect at the silent dynamos. By the same token, the "power room" in our lives is the place where we daily meet and commune with God. During those quiet moments with our Lord, we receive the strength and the power to meet victoriously the challenges of a 20th-century lifestyle.[6]

It was a great day in my life when I discovered that there is no demand made upon my life which isn't a demand upon the life of Christ in me. This is where every one of us should be if we are to know the secret of the rest of faith in Christ.

# Exodus 16:1-36

And they journeyed from Elim, and all the congregation of the Children of Israel came to the Wilderness of Sin, which is between Elim and Sinai, on the fifteenth day of the second month after they departed from the land of Egypt.

Then the whole congregation of the Children of Israel murmured against Moses and Aaron in the wilderness. And the Children of Israel said to them, "Oh, that we had died by the hand of the Lord in the land of Egypt, when we sat by the pots of meat and when we ate bread to the full! For you have brought us out into this wilderness to kill this whole assembly with hunger."

Then the Lord said to Moses, "Behold, I will rain bread from heaven for you. And the people shall go out and gather a certain quota every day, that I may test them, whether they will walk in My law or not. And it shall be on the sixth day that they shall prepare what they bring in, and it shall be twice as much as they gather daily." . . .

So it was that quails came up at evening and covered the camp, and in the morning the dew lay all around the camp. And when the layer of dew lifted, there, on the surface of the wilderness, was a small round substance as fine as frost on the ground.

So when the Children of Israel saw it, they said to one another, "What is it?" For they did not know what it was.

And Moses said to them, "This is the bread which the Lord has given you to eat. This is the thing which the Lord has commanded: 'Let every man gather it according to each one's need, one omer for each person, according to the number of persons; let every man take for those who are in his tent.'"

And the Children of Israel did so and gathered, some more, some less. . . .

So they gathered it every morning, every man according to his need. And when the sun became hot, it melted. And so it was on the sixth day, that they gathered twice as much bread, two omers for each one. And all the rulers of the congregation came and told Moses. . . .

Now it happened that some of the people went out on the seventh day to gather, but they found none.

And the Lord said to Moses, "How long do you refuse to keep My commandments and My laws? See! For the Lord has given you the Sabbath: therefore He gives you on the sixth day bread for two days.

So the people rested on the seventh day. And the house of Israel called its name manna. And it was like white coriander seed, and the taste of it was like wafers made with honey. . . .

And Moses said to Aaron, "Take a pot and put an omer of manna in it, and lay it up before the Lord, to be kept for your generations." As the Lord commanded Moses, so Aaron laid it up before the Testimony, to be kept.

And the Children of Israel ate manna forty years, until they came to an inhabited land; they ate manna until they came to the border of the land of Canaan. Now an omer is one-tenth of an ephah.

# 4
## THE PLACE OF
# EATING

Following the restfulness of security and sufficiency at Elim, the Children of Israel "journeyed . . . and . . . came to the wilderness of Sin" (Ex. 16:1). This particular stage of the journey emphasizes the strength of Moses' faith. For the first time, the full privation and desolation of the desert was etched in the people's minds. Every step they took now led them farther away from food, water, and life. It is not surprising, therefore, that "the whole congregation of the Children of Israel murmured against Moses and Aaron in the wilderness" (v. 2). To them, this was the place of hunger and death. But God, in His marvelous grace, met this need and declared, "Behold, I will rain bread from heaven for you" (v. 4). He made the wilderness of Sin a place of eating.

It is reassuring to know that even when we murmur against the Lord He graciously meets our need—not because of our sin, but in spite of it. His answer to spiritual hunger is "bread from heaven." He provides a place of eating in this wilderness world.

In John 6 the Saviour speaks of Himself as "the living bread which came down from heaven" (v. 51), and in 1 Corinthians 10:3 Paul reminds us that the Children of Israel ate "spiritual food." This, then, is God's provision for us.

## Appearance of the Manna

The Bible gives a precise description of the appearance of this food. "And in the morning, you shall see the glory of the Lord. . . . And when the layer of dew lifted, there, on the surface of the wilderness, was a small round substance, as fine as the frost on the ground" (Ex. 16:7, 14). To understand the significance of the appearance of the manna, we need to observe the manner of the appearance. The dew, in Scripture, is always an emblem of the Holy Spirit, so it is not surprising to learn that the manna never appeared without the presence of the dew. Likewise, the Lord Jesus is never made real to the believer's heart through the Word without the vibrant ministry of the Holy Spirit. Paul puts it perfectly when he says, "But we all, with unveiled face beholding as in a mirror the glory of the Lord, are being transformed into the same Image from glory to glory, just as by the Spirit of the Lord" (2 Cor. 3:18). The supreme purpose of divine revelation is to unveil the Saviour to our hungry souls, in order that we might feed on Him by faith in our hearts with thanksgiving.

Now, the meaning of the appearance is this: When the Children of Israel saw the provision of God, they called it manna, which means in the Hebrew, *What is it?* and in the Chaldean language, *It is a gift* or *a portion.* In our English understanding, it just simply means bread.

In Exodus 16:11-31 and Numbers 11:1-9 it will be noted in every detail that the manna speaks of Christ as the Bread of Life. From the picture in these passages it can be seen that it was *small,* speaking of the humility of Christ: He "made Himself of no reputation" (Phil. 2:7). Further, the manna was round, speaking of the perfection of Christ: "The only begotten of the Father, full of grace and truth" (John 1:14). The manna was *white,* speaking of the holiness of Christ: He was "holy, harmless, undefiled, separate from sinners" (Heb. 7:26). Continuing the description, the manna was *as the frost,* speaking of the freshness of Christ: "The words that I speak to you are spirit, and they are life" (John 6:63). The manna was like *coriander seed,* speaking of the fragrance of Christ. Solomon writes that His name is "ointment poured forth" (Song 1:3). It was as "the taste of pastry prepared with oil" (Num. 11:8), speaking of the authority of Christ, the Anointed One. "For He whom God has sent speaks the words of God, for God does not give the Spirit by measure" (John 3:34). As for taste, manna was like *wafers made with honey,* speaking of the sweetness of Christ: "I sat down in his shade with great delight, and his fruit was sweet to my taste" (Song 2:3). Completing the graphics, manna was like the *color of bdellium* (Num. 11:7), speaking of the preciousness of Christ. Peter reminds us that "to you who believe, He is precious" (1 Peter 2:7). What a comprehensive picture this is of our Lord Jesus Christ! The Holy Spirit reveals Him as we study the Word of God. Our Lord's sufficiency is poetically set forth by J.S.B. Monsell:

I hunger and I thirst; Jesu, my manna be;
Ye living waters, burst out of the rock for me.
Thou bruised and broken Bread, my lifelong wants supply,
As living souls are fed, O, feed me, or I die.[1]

## Abundance of the Manna
We must not overlook the abundance of this bread from heaven. "Then the Lord said to Moses, 'Behold, I will rain bread from heaven for you'" (Ex. 16:4). What a vivid descrip-

tion this is of the abundance of God's provision! We cannot ponder these words without concluding that God's provision was a miraculous abundance. The manna was not a product of the earth; it was not something which Israel brought with them out of Egypt. It was, rather, the provision of God from heaven.

Various attempts have been made to explain away the supernatural character of the manna. In fact, some have tried to identify it with the tamarisk manna, which is found on some of the desert shrubs; but the fact that God's provision fell from heaven and came in such abundance at all times of the year indisputably proves that it was a miraculous provision.

Even though there was an abundance, the Lord gave a specific command as to the distribution of the manna: "Let every man gather it according to each one's need, one omer for each person." Now a conservative estimate of the total number of Israelites who came out of Egypt would be about 2 million. An omer is equivalent to 6 pints; therefore, there would be about 12 million pints, or 9 million pounds, or 4,500 tons gathered daily. To dramatize and emphasize this even further, someone has worked out that 10 trains, each having 30 cars and each car having in it 15 tons, would be needed for a single day's supply. It was a miracle; it was abundant.

We must be aware that God can certainly provide in any way He chooses; often He chooses human instruments to meet needs. A beautiful example is seen in the story of William Burton and his wife who were missionaries in Africa. Mrs. Burton was very ill and often expressed her longing for an orange; citrus fruit of any kind would have been good for her. The nearest orange trees were in an orchard owned by a Mr. Crawford which was a 21 days' jungle trek distance from their station. As Burton left to preach, depressed that he could not provide the needed fruit, Mrs. Burton began to pray that God would meet this need. When Mr. Burton returned, he found that the Lord had answered his wife's prayer—by her bedside was a full basket of oranges. It had happened in this way: Mr. Crawford and his wife had been picking half-ripe oranges and were impressed to send some over to Mrs. Burton. By the time the African helper made the long journey, the delightful, now-ripe oranges were ready to be enjoyed. They were delivered as Mrs. Burton was praying for them and while her husband was preaching the Word. That night the two missionaries rejoiced as they recalled the Lord's promise, "Before they call, I will answer; and while they are still speaking, I will hear" (Isa. 65:24).[2] In this case, God chose to provide through persons sensitive to the inner promptings of the Spirit.

The Scriptures are explicit with regard to the duration of the heavenly manna; there was a continuous abundance. God provided for the Children of Israel for 40 years! It is a comfort to know that God has provided not only a miraculous means of abundance, but also a continuous abundance for our entire lifetime. Even after we have no further need for manna, the Word of God becomes to us grain in the land of Canaan. The Word of God is completely inexhaustible in time and in eternity. We shall never plumb the depth of the meaning and richness for our spiritual need; it is one of the principles of the kingdom.

## Allowance of the Manna

God made stipulations as to the allowance of this bread from heaven. "This is the thing which the Lord has commanded: 'Let every man gather it according to each one's need'" (Ex. 16:16). Given here are some very practical instructions which demand careful attention. While there is an abundance of spiritual nourishment for every true believer, the allowance is not only to be carefully measured, but also prayerfully treasured.

Observe specifically that the manna was to be gathered early. "In the morning . . . you shall see the glory of the Lord" (v. 7). There is a well-known rule for daily devotions: "No Bible, no breakfast." Ted Rendall says, "While the Bible gives no rules for the daily quiet time—when we gather our portion of heavenly manna, there are many examples of godly people who got up early to feed their souls. There is really no substitute for that habit."

We must continually emphasize the need to meet the Lord before the distractions and responsibilities of a new day prevent our doing so. We cannot study any of the Old Testament characters without being impressed again and again that they were men who rose up early to meet their God, and the ultimate New Testament example is that of our Lord Jesus Christ, of whom it is written: "Now in the morning, having risen a long while before daylight, He went out and departed to a solitary place; and there He prayed" (Mark 1:35).

Perhaps it would help us to think about Ralph Spaulding Cushman's words in *The Secret:*

> I met God in the morning
> When my day was at its best,
> And His presence came like sunrise,
> Like a glory in my breast.
>
> All day long the Presence lingered,
> All day long He stayed with me,
> And we sailed in perfect calmness
> O'er a very troubled sea.
>
> Other ships were blown and battered
> Other ships were sore distressed,

But the winds that seemed to drive them
Brought to us a peace and rest.

Then I thought of other mornings,
With a keen remorse of mind,
When I too had loosed the moorings,
With the Presence left behind.

So I think I know the secret,
Learned from many a troubled way:
You must seek Him in the morning
If you want Him through the day![3]

God has something to say in this passage about attitude: the manna was to be humbly gathered. "On the surface of the wilderness, was a small round substance, as fine as the frost *on the ground*" (Ex. 16:14). The manna did not grow on the trees but fell on the ground. In order to obtain it, the Children of Israel had to go down on their knees.

G. Campbell Morgan tells of the way in which the Lord dealt with his attitude as he was in prayer. He felt the Lord was saying to him, "Which do you want to be—a servant of Mine or a great preacher?" Struggling with the question, he asked, "May I not be both, Lord?" He had visions of being an unknown minister in some obscure town. But evaluating the options, Morgan submissively prayed, "O Lord, my greatest wish is to be a servant of Thine." Time has proved that the Lord's response was to make him one of the greatest preachers of recent memory.[4]

Another example, perhaps, will indelibly inscribe the necessity of a humble spirit upon our thought patterns. Entering a hotel in America, a thirsty commercial traveler noticed a drinking fountain with the invitation: "Stoop and drink." When he reached it, he put out his hand to turn on the water, but found no handle. Then he looked for a button to press or a plug to switch on, but found none. The invitation seemed to mock him. Seeing no other way, he then stooped and, as he did so, the cold, clear water flowed and he was able to drink. The fountain was controlled by an electric eye so arranged that when a certain beam of light was interrupted, a switch was operated which opened the faucet.[5]

There is only one approach to the Word of God, and that is on our knees in utter dependence upon our Lord, in a spirit of prayerfulness and humility. For those who do not believe that God is interested in and involved with the minute details of our lives, these Scriptures should dispel the very thought. God instructed His ancient people that the manna was to be gathered daily. "And Moses said, 'Let no one leave any of it till morning.' . . . And the children of Israel did so and gathered, some more, some less" (vv. 19, 17).

The unique thing about it is that God matched the supply to every man's daily need. The man who gathered more found it was reduced to his requirement, and the person who gathered less found it met his need.

There is a great lesson to be learned from the *daily* supply of manna. In studying the account of the manna, the students of Rabbi Simeon ben Jachai asked him why the Lord did not give enough manna to Israel for a year at a time. The Rabbi answered with a parable: "Once there was a king who had a son to whom he gave a yearly allowance, paying him the entire sum on a fixed day. It soon happened that the day on which the allowance was due was the only day of the year the father saw his son. So the king changed his plan and gave the son, day by day, that which sufficed for the day. And now the son visited the father every morning. Thus did God with Israel."[6]

So it is that God meets our daily needs through His Word. In this connection, it must be noticed that those who did not appropriate what was their daily need and left it till the morning discovered that it "bred worms, and stank" (v. 20). It is significant that the Children of Israel who did this were characterized by disobedience as the record tells us: "Notwithstanding they did not heed Moses. But some of them left part of it until morning, and it bred worms, and stank. And Moses was angry with them" (v. 20).

Failure to obey truth, we know produces the same staleness in our Christian experience. As Paul instructs, "Knowledge puffs up, but love edifies" (1 Cor. 8:1). The hallmark of a committed Christian should be *each day we must obey.*

The only exception to the procedure of gathering manna daily was on the sixth day when the Children of Israel had to gather a double portion to eliminate the necessity of gathering on the Sabbath day. "'This,'" Moses commanded, "'is what the Lord has said: Tomorrow is a Sabbath rest, a holy Sabbath to the Lord. Bake what you will bake today, and boil what you will boil, and lay up for yourselves all that remains to be kept until morning'" (Ex. 16:23).

I wonder how many of us prepare ourselves in this fashion for what we now call the Lord's Day. What a difference it would make to our worship and witness if our Bible study prepared us for unhurried meditation and contemplation throughout the Lord's Day! It is this discipline which leads to the depth of experience achieved by Brother Lawrence. He must have longed for the same relationship for others when he wrote, "I cannot imagine how religious persons can live satisfied without the practice of the presence of God."[7]

## Assurance of the Manna
It is characteristic of God to care for His people as evidenced in the assurance of this bread from heaven. "And Moses said

to Aaron, 'Take a pot, and put an omer of manna in it . . . to be kept for your generations'" (v. 33).

The writer to the Hebrews tells us that in the ark of the covenant, overlaid with gold, there was found "the golden pot that had the manna, Aaron's rod that budded, and the tablets of the covenant" (Heb. 9:4). Any Israelite who had doubts as to whether the supply of manna was going to last had only to ask Moses or Aaron about that omer of manna laid up before the Lord.

Now the unusual thing is that while the allowance for each day was completely consumed, the Lord's portion never failed. The manna in the golden pot speaks of Christ in all the power of His risen and glorified life. Indeed, each article in that holy ark speaks of the *aliveness* of our Saviour. There was the living Word—the tablets of the covenant; the living rod—the rod that budded; and the living bread—the golden pot that contained manna.

As long as Jesus lives, we have no fear regarding the divine supply. This is why the Saviour says to the church at Pergamos: "To him who overcomes I will give some of the hidden manna to eat" (Rev. 2:17). This is our assurance that Christ is both the living and the lasting bread from heaven.

What an answer the manna was to the emptiness which the Children of Israel found in the wilderness of Sin. Likewise, as we pass through the wilderness of emptiness on our way to heaven, we can be assured of God's miraculous and continuous supply of the bread from heaven.

# Exodus 17:5-16

And the Lord said to Moses, "Go on before the people, and take with you some of the elders of Israel. Also take in your hand your rod with which you struck the river, and go. Behold, I will stand before you there on the rock in Horeb; and you shall strike the rock, and water will come out of it, that the people may drink." And Moses did so in the sight of the elders of Israel.

So he called the name of the place Massah and Meribah, because of the contention of the Children of Israel, and because they tempted the Lord, saying, "Is the Lord among us or not?"

Now Amalek came and fought with Israel in Rephidim. And Moses said to Joshua, "Choose us some men and go out, fight with Amalek. Tomorrow I will stand on the top of the hill with the rod of God in my hand."

So Joshua did as Moses said to him, and fought with Amalek. And Moses, Aaron, and Hur went up to the top of the hill. And so it was, when Moses held up his hand, that Israel prevailed; and when he let down his hand, Amalek prevailed.

But Moses' hands became heavy; so they took a stone and put it under him, and he sat on it. And Aaron and Hur supported his hands, one on one side, and the other on the other side; and his hands were steady until the going down of the sun. So Joshua defeated Amalek and his people with the edge of the sword.

Then the Lord said to Moses, "Write this for a memorial in the book and recount it in the hearing of Joshua, that I will utterly blot out the remembrance of Amalek from under heaven."

And Moses built an altar and called its name, The-Lord-Is-My-Banner; for he said, "Because the Lord has sworn: the Lord will have war with Amalek from generation to generation."

# 5

## THE PLACE OF

# *FIGHTING*

If, like the Children of Israel, we have been delivered from the bondage of Egypt and separated unto God for a life of worship and witness, we can expect to be attacked by the enemy. If we know nothing about the clash of battle—if we are not conscious of the intensity of the conflict—then we need to ask ourselves if we are really Christians at all!

### The Battle Is Imperious
Three aspects of this warfare are illustrated in this passage from Exodus. The first is that this holy war is imperious. "Now Amalek came and fought with Israel in Rephidim" (Ex. 17:8). This holy war is imperative, urgent, and compelling. No one can be a Christian and seek to live a committed life without encountering an enemy named Amalek. This will become apparent as we see the significance of the enemy's appearance. The Children of Israel had been delivered from Egypt and had passed through the Red Sea (speaking of redemption by blood and by power). They were on their way to God's full purpose of blessing for them in Canaan. At this point, they

could find no water to drink and they complained to Moses. In fact, the place was called "Chiding" or "Tempting," because they tempted the Lord.

Moses, therefore, sought the Lord on behalf of the people and was instructed to go to the rock in Horeb and smite it with the rod of God. This he did in the presence of the elders, and out of the rock gushed the water which became their very life and sustenance throughout the rest of their journey.

Paul, writing about this same event says, "That Rock was Christ" (1 Cor. 10:4). He was the One smitten of God in order that blood and water might flow for our redemption and regeneration. In the blood we see a picture of Calvary, while the water reminds us of Pentecost.

As soon as the rock was smitten and the people had appropriated the water, Amalek appeared. Herein is a parable of spiritual experience. The Bible teaches and church history confirms that when men and women put their faith in the Lord Jesus Christ, experience the cleansing of the blood and the indwelling of the Spirit, the spiritual battle begins. Amalek appears!

G. H. C. MacGregor declares, "When by the reception of the fullness of the Holy Ghost, we have become better fitted to do the work, it becomes the more necessary for the devil to seek to destroy our power. A worldly, inactive, useless Christian, he can afford to leave in peace; a consecrated, Spirit-filled Christian, he must withstand to the utmost. The higher we rise into the light of God, the better target do we present to the shafts of the enemy. After times of ecstasy come times of temptation."[1]

Amalek represents the flesh. He was of the seed of Esau, the carnally minded man who sold his birthright for a mess of pottage; who walked the way of the flesh and lost his inheritance. Amalek was always found *inside* the Israelites' camp.

The Word of God makes it clear that the enemies of the

Christian are the world, the flesh, and the devil. Perhaps our greatest enemy is the flesh because the devil rarely attacks us unless it is through the flesh. Nor does the world allure us except through the flesh. From the moment of our new birth, there is a battle between the flesh and the Spirit.

Charles L. Allen writes, "God gave to each person power of choice and freedom of will. We remember how our Lord prayed, 'Nevertheless not My will, but Yours, be done' (Luke 22:42). That prayer teaches two very important truths: first, one might have a will for his own life that is contrary to God's will for him; second, it is possible to follow your own will and turn your back on God's will for you."[2] Paul wrote, "For the flesh lusts against the Spirit, and the Spirit against the flesh; and these are contrary to one another" (Gal. 5:17). It follows, therefore, that if we are to know spiritual victory, then we must conquer Amalek.

This holy war is further imperious because of the seriousness of the enemy's antagonism. Lloyd John Ogilvie aptly states that whenever Christ "is at work in us in our character, that's when Satan builds up his forces of resistance. Once Christ calls us to be His person, the battle begins. As Christ moves into all the areas of our lives to make us totally His and more and more like Him, we can be sure that Satan will dig in and resist that invasion at those points where we are the most vulnerable."[3]

There is no misunderstanding the Scripture: "The Lord has sworn: the Lord will have war with Amalek from generation to generation" (Ex. 17:16). The marginal rendering precedes this with the words, "Because the hand of Amalek is against the throne of the Lord." The flesh within us is the sworn enemy of God. "The carnal mind is enmity against God; for it is not subject to the Law of God, nor indeed can be" (Rom. 8:7).

There is a deadly conflict, a sworn variance, between the

Spirit and the flesh; an antagonism that cannot be settled. Even if the flesh retreats for a time, it will emerge as a sleeping giant, awakened to destroy the home, split the church, or damage our service for God in the world.

We must be aware that this holy war is imperious also because of the subtleness of the enemy's attacks. Moses recalls the period when the Children of Israel passed through Rephidim. "Remember what Amalek did to you on the way as you were coming out of Egypt; how he met you on the way and attacked your rear ranks, all the stragglers at your rear, when you were tired and weary, and he did not fear God" (Deut. 25:17-18).

Satan never attacks face to face, but always tries to catch a person unaware. When the Children of Israel were faint and weary and not maintaining the pace, Amalek came upon them and smote them.

This is exactly what is happening continually in the church. The enemy attacks the people who are on the periphery—the weak and backslidden ones—and we see them go down before our very eyes. Ted Rendall indicates that this is what happened to King David. "It is clear from the biblical record that David should not have been in Jerusalem on that fateful evening when the flesh conquered the giant killer. David was drawn away by his own lust and mastered by it. The lust of the flesh is always subtle, catching us unaware and totally defeating us."[4]

## The Battle Is Continuous

To understand the seriousness of the matter, we must grapple with the fact that this holy war is continuous. From the moment Amalek struck his first blow until now, the fight has been continuous. It is a day-long battle. The battle went on "until the going down of the sun" (Ex. 17:12). An enemy who is prepared to fight until sundown is a vicious foe. These sons of Esau could have given up at certain points in the day, as would other enemies, but not so the Amalekites. This lesson applies to us today. At any moment, the bow is bent; the arrow is poised on the string; the enemy is ready to attack.

Since this war is continuous, we must expect it to be an agelong battle. "The Lord will have war with Amalek from generation to generation" (v. 16). They harassed the Children of Israel under Joshua, under Saul, under David; the battle still goes on in the land of Palestine today. The struggle between the Arabs and the Jews will never be stopped. Until God winds up earth's affairs, the battle will go on from generation to generation.

## The Battle Is Victorious

"And so it was, when Moses held up his hand, that Israel prevailed; and when he let down his hand, Amalek prevailed" (v. 11). What is the secret of victory against Amalek? To put it simply, it is first of all, dependence upon a life of power. "Moses said to Joshua, 'Choose us some men and go out; fight with Amalek'" (v. 9). The name Joshua means *saviour* or *deliverer*. In fact, the name Jesus is the New Testament equivalent for Joshua. Therefore, Joshua represents Christ's power energizing the believer. Notice, however, that Christ operates only through chosen people; in other words, through dedicated, disciplined, and devoted men and women. The life of power is dependent upon complete submission and surrender to the indwelling Christ.

Some years ago a full-page picture appeared in *Life* magazine of the devastation wrought by a midwestern tornado. In the center of the picture was a telephone pole with a straw driven through it. It seemed incredible! How could a flimsy, insubstantial straw be thrust through a rugged, seasoned telephone pole? Here's the answer: the straw was utterly surrendered to the tornado and its awesome power. The weakest of God's children, when utterly surrendered to the Spirit of God, can bring to pass things which are humanly impossible."[5]

But even though Joshua and his chosen men were armed and ready to fight, there was still the possibility of defeat. The record tells that "when Moses held up his hand . . . Israel prevailed; and when he let down his hand, Amalek prevailed" (v. 11). Impending defeat brings into focus the need for a life of prayer. "Moses' hands became heavy; so they took a stone and put it under him, and he sat on it. And Aaron and Hur supported his hands, one on one side, and the other on the other side" (v. 12).

Aaron represents the priesthood of believers and the life of prayer. It was he who brought the intercession of the people before God. Moses is a symbol of our Lord Jesus Christ enthroned in heaven. Jesus Christ is our great leader, who has pioneered the way of faith. "We see Jesus . . . crowned with glory and honor" (Heb. 2:9). We not only have Christ in us, we have Christ for us because "He is also able to save to the uttermost those who come to God through Him, since He ever lives to make intercession for them" (7:25).

But even Christ on the throne doesn't mediate His power without His Aarons. Prayer is dependent upon the Aarons here on earth. Even though He is sovereign and omnipotent, Christ the Lord counts on His people for the implementation of His intercessory mediations and ministrations. John Wesley affirms, "God does nothing but in answer to prayer."[6] I cannot explain this but it is true; otherwise, there is no purpose in prayer whatsoever.

In his book, *Destined for the Throne,* Dr. Paul E. Billheimer writes, "The authority over Satan and his hierarchy which Christ delegated to His Church operates wholly within the framework and system of believing prayer which God has ordained. By God's own choice, all of this vast delegated authority is wholly inoperative apart from the prayers of a believing Church. If the church does not pray God will not act, because that would nullify His plan to prepare her for rulership through 'on-the-job' training in enforcing Christ's victory at Calvary. If it were not for His determination to bring her up to full stature as His co-regent, God would not have established the system of prayer at all. There is not intrinsic power in prayer as such. On the contrary, prayer is an acknowledgment of need, of helplessness. If He chose, He could act arbitrarily without regard to prayer or lack of it. All power originates in God and belongs to Him alone. *He ordained prayer not primarily as a means of getting things done for Himself, but as part of the apprenticeship program for training the church for her royal duties which will follow the Marriage Supper of the Lamb. Unless she understands this and enters into sincere cooperation with God's plan of prayer, the power needed to overcome and bind Satan on earth will not be released.* God has the power to overcome Satan without the cooperation of His church through prayer and faith, but if He did it without her it would deprive her of enforcement practice and rob her of the strength she would gain in overcoming. This is God's primary reason for inaugurating the system of prayer and unequivocally binding Himself to answer. *Therefore, there is no authority apart from persistent believing prayer."* [7]

So we see that the life of power is dependent upon the life of prayer; and, in turn, the life of prayer is dependent upon a life of purity. "Hur supported his hands" (Ex. 17:12), our text says. Hur was the grandfather of Bezaleel, the artificer and sculptor who made practically everything for the tabernacle in the wilderness. His name means *whiteness* or *purity*. Whenever Hur appears in Scripture, he is associated with that which is holy.

The lesson is this—prayer is canceled out where there is no holiness. The psalmist cries, "If I regard iniquity in my heart, the Lord will not hear" (Ps. 66:18). Writing to Timothy, Paul pleads, "Therefore I desire that the men pray everywhere, lifting up holy hands" (1 Tim. 2:8).

Arthur W. Pink observes, "Hur means light—the emblem of divine holiness, *and* so points to the Holy Spirit of God."[8] It is only the Holy Spirit through the Holy Scriptures who can make us effective in prayer. "Likewise the Spirit also helps in our weaknesses. For we do not know what we should pray for as we ought, but the Spirit Himself makes intercession for us with groanings which cannot be uttered. Now He who searches the hearts knows what the mind of the Spirit is, because He makes intercession for the saints according to the will of God" (Rom. 8:26-27).

It follows, therefore, that if there are no uplifted hands of Hur, Aaron's ministry is powerless. And if Aaron's ministry fails, Joshua fails. It is a chain reaction. These essential elements of victory—the life of power, the life of prayer, and the life of purity—are inseparably bound together. Our risen Lord requires all three for the *continuous* defeat of Amalek.

Some may object to what I have said about the *continuous* defeat of Amalek. I am not unmindful of such verses as Romans 6:11, 2 Timothy 2:22, and other similar passages. But there are other Scriptures which present the other side of the picture. There is a fight to be fought. (See 1 Tim. 6:12; 2 Tim. 4:7.) This fight has to do with the *flesh.* The Apostle Paul was clear on this. He could testify: "Thus I fight: not as one who beats the air. But I discipline my body and bring it into subjection, lest, when I have preached to others, I myself should become disqualified" (1 Cor. 9:26-27).

This fight continued right to the end of his life when he affirmed, "I have fought the good fight; I have finished the race; I have kept the faith" (2 Tim. 4:7). In like manner, we can be victorious notwithstanding the imperious and continuous warfare in which we are engaged. The secret is our union with our heavenly Moses on the throne. As we live in fellowship with Him through lives of purity and prayer, the power for victory flows and Amalek is defeated.

Make no mistake about it, going places with God brings us inevitably to the place of fighting. Most Christians do not want to be reminded of this. They would sooner merge with the confused and compromising world. Indeed, the situation identifies with Horatius Bonar (1808-89), the Scottish minister who lamented, "I looked for the church, I found it in the world; I looked for the world, I found it in the church." This grieves our risen and reigning Lord. He waits to see His Kingdom come and His will done on earth as it is in heaven. But His divine purposes will be frustrated until we are willing to "fight the fight of faith." The power to win is available and adequate. He wants men and women of purity and prayer who are ready to answer the *call* to arms.

# Exodus 33:12-23

Then Moses said to the Lord, "See, You say to me, 'Bring up this people.' But You have not let me know whom You will send with me. Yet You have said, 'I know you by name, and you have also found grace in My sight.'

"Now therefore, I pray, if I have found grace in Your sight, show me now Your way, that I may know You and that I may find grace in Your sight. And consider that this nation is Your people."

And He said, "My Presence will go with you, and I will give you rest."

Then he said to Him, "If Your Presence does not go with us, do not bring us up from here. For how then will it be known that Your people and I have found grace in Your sight, except You go with us? So we shall be separate, Your people and I, from all the people who are upon the face of the earth."

Then the Lord said to Moses, "I will also do this thing that you have spoken; for you have found grace in My sight, and I know you by name."

And he said, "Please, show me Your glory."

Then He said, "I will make all My goodness pass before you, and I will proclaim the name of the Lord before you. I will be gracious to whom I will be gracious, and I will have compassion on whom I will have compassion.

But He said, "You cannot see My face; for no man shall see Me and live."

And the Lord said, "Here is a place by Me, and you shall stand on the rock. So it shall be, while My glory passes by, that I will put you in a cleft of the rock, and will cover you with My hand while I pass by. Then I will take away My hand, and you shall see My back; but My face shall not be seen."

# 6

## THE PLACE OF

# *LEADING*

Moses, the servant of the Lord, was in great difficulty. He was being confronted with rebellion, idolatry, and sin in the camp of Israel. Before he could possibly continue with his solemn and serious responsibility, he must be assured of the presence and blessing of Almighty God. He came, therefore, before Jehovah and said: "Now therefore, I pray, if I have found grace in Your sight, show me now Your way, that I may know You and I may find grace in Your sight. And consider that this nation is Your people" (Ex. 33:13). God's reply to this impassioned appeal is one of the great and glorious promises of the Bible—"My Presence will go with you and I will give you rest" (v. 14). Here was the commendation of the divine presence and, inherently, the intimacy of His fellowship. A more literal translation is, "I Myself will go with you."

## The Commendation of the Divine Presence
It is comforting to know that whatever our circumstances, God will be with us and we can experience the intimacy of His fellowship. David knew something of this when he wrote what

we now call the 23rd Psalm. "Yea, though I walk through the valley of the shadow of death, I will fear no evil; for You are with me" (Ps. 23:4). It has often been pointed out that in the earlier verses of this psalm, David uses the third person to identify the Shepherd: "He makes me to lie down in green pastures; He leads me beside the still waters. He restores my soul; He leads me in the paths of righteousness For His name's sake" (vv. 2-3). But when the valley of the shadow of death is reached, with all its trial and testing, the third person is changed to the second person. David declares, "I will fear no evil; for You are with me" (v. 4). As someone has insightfully remarked, there is not even room for the verb "to be" because the phrase in the original reads, "You are with me." Such is the intimacy of His fellowship, especially in times of darkness and distress.

F. W. Boreham recounts that in 1896, Glasgow University conferred on Dr. David Livingstone the degree of Doctor of Laws. "As Dr. Livingstone rose to speak he was received in respectful silence." Boreham continues, "He was gaunt, haggard as a result of hardships in tropical Africa, his left arm crushed by a lion, hanging helplessly at his side [as] he announced his resolve to return to Africa, without misgiving and with great gladness. He added, 'Would you like me to tell you what supported me through all the years of exile among a people whose language I could not understand, and whose attitude toward me was always uncertain and often hostile? It was this, 'Lo, I am with you always, even to the end of the age.' On these words I staked everything, and they never failed.' He had the companionship of the Son of God."[1]

There is the intimacy of His fellowship, but there is also the radiancy of His face. "I Myself with My face will go with you," is another translation. This was a familiar expression to the Children of Israel. When God's face was upon His people, it was a sign of His approval and benediction. On the other hand, when there was no light of His countenance, then it was an evidence of His displeasure and judgment.

If we know the intimacy of His fellowship we shall also have the radiancy of His face. The words of W. Spencer Walton are as meaningful today as when written by this 19th-century missionary:

I've seen the face of Jesus—He smiled in love on me;
It filled my heart with rapture, my soul with ecstasy.
The scars of deepest anguish were lost in glory bright;
I've seen the face of Jesus—it was a wondrous sight.

And since I've seen His beauty, all else I count but loss;
The world, its fame and pleasure, is now to me but dross.
His light dispelled my darkness, His smile was, Oh, so sweet!
I've seen the face of Jesus—I can but kiss His feet.[2]

His face is as a light upon our path—all other lights pale by comparison. Solomon affirms in those now-familiar words: "The path of the just is like the shining sun, that shines ever brighter unto the perfect day" (Prov. 4:18). And the Lord Jesus says, "He who follows Me shall not walk in darkness, but have the light of life" (John 8:12). The Father has not promised us an easy path, but He has assured us a lighted path.

In *Tell No Man,* Adela Rogers St. Johns' main character describes his conversion to Christ in terms of light as he sat on the shore of Lake Michigan: "A radiance began to glow on the water. *That's not metaphorical,* it's a fact in my life. Out of those leaden skies, a star melted the mist, the surface of the water was lighted up, *my* world was filled with light . . . try to imagine all the light and all the kinds of light beyond and beyond, so much farther beyond . . . . Just as it had done away with the blackness and damp air outside, the darkness and despair and *hopelessness* and all the bitter questions *inside* me were gone. I was—*new* . . . the joy was as much beyond any joy I'd ever dreamed could be as the *light* was beyond and *more* than any light I'd ever seen . . . and yet [the light] was small enough to fit me and for me to have it."[3] We are infused with His light as we relinquish our inner darkness to Him.

To know the intimacy of God's fellowship is to enjoy the radiancy of His face and the sufficiency of His favor. To Moses, that meant the Promised Land—Canaan—the land of "milk and honey" (Ex. 3:8). To us, it symbolizes all the wonderful richness of life in Christ. Among other blessings, this rest speaks of the inner calm and tranquility which is the secret of the people of God. William Nicholson once wrote a letter to a friend . . . and finished up with a characteristic phrase, "Yours restfully, Billy." No Christian can know progress in his spiritual life if there is conflict and frustration. But thank God, we can know rest from the curse of sin and rest from the conflict of self. The Master said, "Come to Me, all you who labor and are heavy laden, and I will give you rest" (Matt. 11:28). This is rest from sin. He also invited, "Take My yoke upon you and learn from Me, for I am gentle and lowly in heart, and you will find rest for your souls" (v. 29). This is rest from self. In other words, the Master offers not only peace with God, but the peace of God. Hymnwriter Edward H. Bickersteth put it beautifully when he wrote:

> Peace, perfect peace,
> By thronging duties pressed?
> To do the will of Jesus—
> This is rest.[4]

The commendation of the divine presence assures us of the intimacy of His fellowship, the radiancy of His face, and the sufficiency of His favor.

## The Confirmation of the Divine Presence

A deeper examination of our text reveals the confirmation of the divine presence. Moses said, "If Your Presence does not go with us, do not bring us up from here. For how then will it be known that Your people and I have found grace in Your sight, except You go with us? So we shall be separate, Your people and I, from all the people who are upon the face of the earth" (Ex. 33:15-16). The confirmation of the divine presence was to be evidenced by a life of separation, involving two aspects of holiness—preservation in the world and dedication to the Lord.

Preservation in the world does not mean isolation so much as it means insulation. They were to be *in* the world, but not *of* it. (For that matter, so are Christians today!) This calls to mind the words of our Lord in His high priestly prayer: "I do not pray that You should take them out of the world, but that You should keep them from the evil one" (John 17:15). In the same chapter are those profound words of our Lord, "Sanctify them by Your truth. Your word is truth" (v. 17). The Apostle Paul wrote, "The God of peace Himself sanctify you completely; and may your whole spirit, soul, and body be preserved blameless at the coming of our Lord Jesus Christ" (1 Thes. 5:23).

Perhaps a parable will crystalize for us the concept of being in the world, but not of the world: The world is like an ocean. In the world we are boats. A boat is only useful in the water: if the boat is in the water, it is useful. If the water is in the boat, it will sink beneath the waves. Therefore, bale out the water.[5]

A separated people is a preserved people, living blamelessly and triumphantly within a contemporary world. Where there is compromise, there is at once the loss of the sense of the Lord's presence.

The second facet of holiness is dedication to the Lord. "And do not present your members as instruments of unrighteousness to sin, but present yourselves to God" (Rom. 6:13). Later on, Paul exhorted, "I beseech you therefore, brethren, by the mercies of God, that you present your bodies a living sacrifice, holy, acceptable to God, which is your reasonable service" (12:1).

Traveling through Germany on his way to Paris, Count Zinzendorf stopped at the town of Düsseldorf, where there was a fine collection of paintings. He went into the art gallery to spend an hour or two admiring the works of some of the great masters. Coming to a picture of Christ suffering on the cross, the young man stood transfixed before the scene as he read the words the artist Steinberg had chosen to interpret the painting: "All this I did for thee. What hast thou done for Me?" It was the turning point of the Count's life. Abandoning his plans to visit Paris, he returned to his home and consecrated himself to the Lord Jesus Christ. Devoting all that he was and all that he possessed to the Master's service, he became the founder of the Moravian brethren.[6] Show me a man who is totally abandoned to God, and I will show you one who practices the presence of Christ and knows "what is that good, and acceptable, and perfect will of God" (Rom. 12:2).

The life of the late Dr. William Culbertson should be an inspiration to us all. Elected to serve as bishop of the New York and Philadelphia Synod of the Reformed Episcopal Church at the age of 21—the youngest man ever to serve in this position—Dr. Culbertson later filled the office of president of Moody Bible Institute for many years. Among his associates, both fellow workers and students, it was often said of him, "He is a man of God."[7] Such a testimony gives evidence to a life committed to going places with God.

## The Compensation of the Divine Presence

Our lives are enriched as we experience the confirmation of the divine presence and magnified as we learn of the compensation of the divine presence. No one can walk with God and feel the power of His nearness without an insatiable longing to see more and more of His glory. David expressed this longing when he cried, "One thing I have desired of the Lord, that will I seek: That I may dwell in the house of the Lord all the days of my life, to behold the beauty of the Lord, and to inquire in His temple" (Ps. 27:4).

A beautiful story is told of Thomas Aquinas, that great theologian of the 13th century. As he came out of his private chapel one memorable morning, looking dazed and dazzled, the young man who was his secretary came to him and inquired, "Father, are you going to dictate this morning?" "No, my brother," was the saintly man's reply, "for all the theology I have ever written seems as but straw in the glory of what I have seen today." What a difference it would make to our enjoyment of the divine presence, if we spent enough time in the presence of God to capture such discerning visions as this!

The deep impressions made on the disciples were those of the glory of God in the face of Jesus Christ. As John writes, "And the Word became flesh and dwelt among us, and we beheld His glory, the glory as of the only begotten of the Father, full of grace and truth" (John 1:14). And the Apostle Paul tells us, "We all, with unveiled face, beholding as in a mirror the glory of the Lord, are being transformed into the same image from glory to glory, just as by the Spirit of the Lord" (2 Cor. 3:18).

"What is the chief end of man?" asked a Scottish minister

of his little daughter. Being a well-instructed child, she replied in familiar words—"To glorify God, and to enjoy Him forever." Wondering how much of that answer his child really understood, the father suddenly put a second question, and one which is not found in the catechism: "And what is the chief end of God?" At once the answer came back: "To glorify man, and to enjoy him forever." Surely that answer was correct![8]

The secret of seeing this divine glory is unfolded to us in the reply that God made to Moses: "I will make all My goodness pass before you, and I will proclaim the name of the Lord before you. I will be gracious to whom I will be gracious, and I will have compassion on whom I will have compassion" (Ex. 33:19). In other words, Moses was to experience the compensation of the divine presence by an appreciation of God's goodness. Glory is the outshining of goodness and goodness is the very nature of God. Moses had to be hidden in the cleft of the rock while God showed him His goodness.

Most commentators agree that the rock was the one which was smitten by Moses when he prayed for water to quench the thirst of the Children of Israel. If that be so, then there is a deep significance here; if we are going to see the glory of God, we must experience the goodness of God. We can only do this as we go deeper into the meaning of the Cross and allow it to be effective in our lives.

A great artist once sought to paint the scene of the Crucifixion. With marvelous skill he sketched the skull-shaped hill crowned by three crosses and with true delineation pictured the two thieves hanging in agony upon their emblems of despair. But when he came to depict the figure upon the central cross, he found that his hand had lost its cunning, and that he was impotent to portray the figure of the world's great Redeemer. Finally, in despair, he simply enveloped the central cross in a sunburst of glory and left it thus. The artist was right. As we gaze upon the cross of Christ we see the goodness of

God in a sunburst of glory.[9]

Once we have developed an appreciation of God's goodness, we are ready for an appropriation of God's grace. In His revelation to Moses God was saying, "This is not something I am going to do specially for you, but this is going to be the privilege of all who will walk with Me, and know My presence, and see My glory." There can be no greater manifestation of the glory of God than through the expression of the grace of God.

How desperately we need God's grace for our justification, our sanctification, and our glorification! Where sin abounds in our lives, there grace must abound in extra proportion if we are going to live in the light of God's glory.

The presence of God is a promise! We have the divine commendation of it, the divine confirmation of it, and the divine compensation of it. We need only submit to Him to receive that constant, abiding presence. To do otherwise is to be impoverished and unblessed. No wonder Moses said, "If Your presence does not go with us, do not bring us up from here" (Ex. 33:15). At that time the problems and testings which confronted Moses looked formidable and filled him with fear; but he was invigorated when God said, "My presence will go with you, and I will give you rest" (v. 14).

It can be so in the life of any Christian or church that knows the glory and blessing of the Lord Jehovah. Remember the words of Jesus: "Go therefore, and make disciples of all the nations, baptizing them in the name of the Father and of the Son and of the Holy Spirit, teaching them to observe all things that I have commanded you; and, lo, I am with you always, even to the end of the age" (Matt. 28:19-20).

May this promised presence of our risen Lord, revealed to Moses, tested through experience, intensified by desire, be the motivation for our thoughts, our attitudes, and our actions.

# Joshua 1:1-9

After the death of Moses the servant of the Lord, it came to pass that the Lord spoke to Joshua, the son of Nun, Moses' assistant, saying: "Moses My servant is dead. Now therefore, arise, go over this Jordan, you and all this people, to the land which I am giving to them—the Children of Israel.

"Every place that the sole of your foot will tread upon I have given you, as I said to Moses. From the wilderness and this Lebanon as far as the great river, the River Euphrates, all the land of the Hittites, and to the great sea toward the going down of the sun, shall be your territory.

"No man shall be able to stand before you all the days of your life; as I was with Moses, so I will be with you. I will not leave you nor forsake you.

"Be strong and of good courage, for to this people you shall divide as an inheritance the land which I swore to their fathers to give them. Only be strong and very courageous, that you may observe to do according to all the Law which Moses My servant commanded you; do not turn from it to the right hand or to the left, that you may prosper wherever you go.

"This Book of the Law shall not depart from your mouth, but you shall meditate in it day and night, that you may observe to do according to all that is written in it. For then you will make your way prosperous, and then you will have good success. Have I not commanded you? Be strong and of a good courage; do not be afraid, nor be dismayed, for the Lord your God is with you wherever you go."

# 7
## THE PLACE OF
# TRUSTING

We come to a turning point as we consider a new man, Joshua. In God's purpose, Joshua was destined to be the leader and deliverer of his people as they marched into Canaan. Joshua had been set apart by God while Moses was still alive. "Take Joshua . . . and set him before . . . all the congregation, and inaugurate him" (Num. 27:18-19).

Joshua was doubtless a child when the Children of Israel came out of Egypt, born of a not-too-well-known family.

As commanding officer he led the attack against the Amalekites. Repeatedly, we read of the confidence that Moses placed in him. Particularly was this so when the 12 spies were sent to look over the land and bring back a report. Ten of them tried to discourage the people from ever entering in, and so effective were they that they created grumbling and complaining among the people until God had to judge them. Not a soul of that generation, save Caleb and Joshua, entered into the land of Canaan. But it was on that occasion that his name was changed from Oshea to Joshua—from *deliverer* to *Jehovah saves*.

## Trust the Purpose of God

The great crisis of Joshua's life has now come. Ted Engstrom helps us to understand the complexity of Joshua's situation through this explanation: "The Chinese language has a word which symbolically typifies our age. As we know, the Chinese language does not use the romanized alphabet as we do in the West, but it is made up of characters. The classical Chinese language has about 48,000 characters, and during the days of Chairman Mao's leadership in Mainland China he arranged for the language to be simplified to 2,800 characters . . . . The character for the word *crisis* in both the classical and simplified Chinese is made up of two smaller characters meaning *danger* and *opportunity*. In an amazing way it appears we are witnessing these two elements in our present day of crisis. We have the trauma of the world's massive problems and difficulties on the one hand, and the indisputable fact that God is mightily at work in His world on the other. In spite of vast and deep darkness, a light shines ever more brightly."[1]

As Joshua walks into the unknown future, laced with danger and opportunity, God meets with him in a message that lifts him above all his fears. Notice that God calls Joshua to trust His purpose. "After the death of Moses the servant of the Lord, it came to pass that the Lord spoke to Joshua the son of Nun, Moses' assistant, saying: 'Moses My servant is dead. Now therefore, arise, go over this Jordan'" (Josh. 1:1-2). The purpose of God is always realistic as well as redemptive. Moses, this mighty man, educated in all the arts of Egypt—a man who brought the Children of Israel out of Egypt under the blood, through the Red Sea, into the wilderness; a man who could intercede with God for the provision of food for the hungry, mobilize 2½ million people, organize and lead the building of the tabernacle for the worship of God; a man who knew how to deal with civil rights and with sociological problems of all kinds within the camp—was dead.

A discerning person once said that the will of God will never lead where the grace of God cannot keep. God never leads us into the place of trusting without making us aware of the testings we have to face. Albert Schweitzer wrote, "The power of ideals is incalculable. We see no power in a drop of water. But let it get into a crack in the rock and be turned to ice, and it splits the rock; turned into steam, it drives the pistons of the most powerful engines. Something has happened to it which makes active and effective the power that is latent in it."[2] The same can be said of learning to trust. Trusting implicitly in God frees one's thinking, releasing creative power to be applied to the situation. Let's look at some of the possibilities that must have been going through Joshua's mind.

Technologically, Joshua was thinking of Canaan. No longer were the Israelites a wandering people; they were about to cross Jordan, conquer Canaan, divide their possessions, and carve homes and cities out of the landscape. And though not as developed as we are today, technologically speaking, Joshua had to do a bit of thinking. Moses was trained in the universities of Egypt. He had built great cities; he had led tremendous conquests—but Moses was dead. Joshua did not have the experience of Moses. Moreover, not a single soul who came out of Egypt, except Caleb, was alive to teach him; and save that which he had learned from Moses and that which he was about to learn from God, he had an unknown land to be developed technologically.

Economically, this colossal crowd had to be fed. Prior to this time, quails had been provided for meat, manna for bread, water out of the rock to drink—but would the quails appear again? Would the manna fall from heaven? How would the population be fed as Israel reached Canaan?

Sociologically, Joshua was confronted with an enormous

problem. He was about to go into a land and hammer out all the social problems: the dividing of the land, the settling of civil rights, the building up of the individual tribes in their own appointed places, with rule and justice carried out according to God's command.

Militaristically, he was facing one of the most gigantic adventures and wars in the history of the Bible. Seven nations were across that Jordan and every one of them had to be conquered. Jericho had to be razed; later Ai, and other cities had to be subdued. Joshua, without anything like the armaments that these nations possessed, had to lead the people of God into battle to take over the land.

Likewise, no thoughtful person can question the grim situation that we face in our contemporary world. The economist is worried about inflation and recession. The ecologist feels the ultimate consequences of a polluted world. The existentialist sees life as a dark tunnel of despair and final extinction. The educationalist has to admit that with all the advance of knowledge in recent years man is inherently and morally unchanged. The ecumenist has had to admit that syncretism has provided no final grounds for unity or victory in a religious world of confusion and paralysis. Whatever we trusted in the past, in terms of history, experience, tradition, law, or principles, there is only one way we can look and that is heavenward. God's purpose is realistic and we've got to face it!

The first step is to say with conviction, "I am no longer anxious about anything, as I realize the Lord is able to carry out His will, and His will is mine. It makes no matter where He places me, or how. That is rather for Him to consider than for me; for in the easiest positions He must give me His grace, and in the most difficult, His grace is sufficient."[3]

The purpose of God is always redemptive. God never brings us into realistic, stark challenge and confrontation without giving us a solution; the solution always comes by identification with our risen Saviour through death in Jordan. Jordan speaks of death to self, of death to everything that *I* represents and life to everything that God represents. It means that the situation before me is so great that I can't look to Moses, I can't look to man. There is only one place to put my problems: bury them in Jordan and look to God for the answer.

Charles R. Brown tells of having seen huge icebergs on the coast of Labrador, towering 300 or 400 feet in the air. These icebergs sail directly south in the teeth of a strong headwind. They have neither sails nor rudder by which they stay on course. But the bulk of the iceberg is under water. The great Labrador current moves strongly southward. It grips the huge bulk of those icebergs and bears them along no matter how the wind may blow on the surface.[4] The Christian too faces powerful headwinds. But when he is caught up in the current of God's redemptive plan for this world, nothing can stop him or divert him from doing God's will.

## Trust the Promises of God

Joshua was compelled to trust God's promises. "Every place that the sole of your foot will tread upon I have given you, as I said to Moses" (Josh. 1:3). God's promises never fail, for God cannot lie. There are only two things that we are to do with them. First, we are to believe them. Do you believe that God who broke into time to feed the Children of Israel with bread; the God who sent quail from nowhere to satisfy the craving of the multitude; the God who spread a table in the wilderness; the God who led His people without guns or munitions to the walls of Jericho and then enabled them to take over a country, is the God who can turn the tides in our country through revival, change the entire attitude of our government, release the abundance and surplus that is so often burned to keep the market down, and do above and beyond that which we could ever ask or think? Can we believe the promises? We must! We must be as confident as Adoniram Judson was when he referred to the missionary work in the Far East: "The prospect is as bright as the promises of God."

Second, we are to receive the promises. So often we *believe* Christ, but we do not *receive* Christ; we *believe* the Word of God, but we do not *receive* the Word of God. To state it plainly, we do not possess our possessions. Do you believe that if there were a number of people in our fast-moving world prepared to pray through the dramatic changes we want to see in our country today that God would bring them about? Do you have the faith to make the nerve center of your own universe a center of prayer?

A dear lady who had been a constant seeker after God for many years had the letters "T" and "P" on many pages of her Bible. A friend asked what the letters represented. "Oh," she said, "they stand for 'tried and proved.' When I have read a promise of God, I try it and prove it, and thank God, I have tried and proved scores of His precious promises!"[5]

## Trust the Power of God

God called Joshua to trust His power. I cannot imagine anything more wonderful than to be told by the Almighty to trust in Him. Thankfully, He has promised that in Christ we can know both victorious power and continuous power.

The city of Jericho was fully armed. Humanly speaking, the Children of Israel did not have a chance; yet they leveled that city. Following that victory they entered Ai, and defeated each of the seven nations in Canaan, took the land, and stepped on the very necks of their kings.

What God did for Joshua, He has done in Christ against principalities and powers; our problem today is not the problem of flesh and blood. Primarily, behind the whole situation confronting us today is a sinister attack by Satan himself. He knows that his time is short. Jesus won the victory for us on the cross; we must learn how to use that victory against the powers of darkness. How wonderful it is to claim the promises: "For the weapons of our warfare are not carnal but mighty in God for pulling down strongholds" (2 Cor. 10:4); "He who is in you is greater than he who is in the world" (1 John 4:4); "If God is for us, who can be against us?" (Rom. 8:31) The triumphant sufficiency of Christ taps the best within us and causes us to experience His victorious power.

God's power does not vacillate. It is constant. Steadfast. Paul flatly states that God "always leads us in triumph" (2 Cor. 2:14). "We are more than conquerors through Him who loved us" (Rom. 8:37). If we are to be in the place of trusting, we must know His purpose, His promise, and His power in our lives.

## Trust the Presence of God
Further, Joshua was to trust the presence of God. "As I was with Moses, so I will be with you. I will not leave you nor forsake you. Be strong and of good courage, for to this people you shall divide as an inheritance the land which I swore to their fathers to give them .... This Book of the Law shall not depart from your mouth, but you shall meditate in it day and night, that you may observe to do according to all that is written in it. For then you will make your way prosperous, and then you will have good success. Have not I commanded you? Be strong and of good courage; do not be afraid, do not be dismayed, for the Lord your God is with you wherever you go" (Josh. 1:5-6, 8-9).

That presence was mediated to Joshua, as it is mediated to us today, through the Word. Alexander Naismith tells that one of his sons, attending a school in Great Britain for the first time, came home saying that he was to write a short essay on "My Greatest Treasure." Naismith wondered what his small son would choose to write about. When he saw the finished composition, he was delighted that the first sentence was, "My greatest treasure is my Holy Bible."[6]

What was Joshua to do with the Book? First of all, he was to *love* the Book. At one time Charles Spurgeon was in Scotland and came across a very old, much-worn Bible. As he held it reverently in his hand, turning it first one way and then another, he noticed a small hole where a worm had eaten its way from cover to cover. He saw a parallel that so excited him that he exclaimed, "Lord, make me a bookworm like that . . . from Genesis to Revelation it has gone clear through the Bible."[7]

We do not have men today who speak with authority out of the Book. The Bible declares, "Righteousness exalts a nation, but sin is a reproach to any people" (Prov. 14:34). That is true nationally, as well as individually. Joshua's attitude toward the Word of God was that he was to love the Book.

He was also to *learn* the Book. "You shall meditate in it day and night" (Joshua 1:8). The word *meditate* literally means to digest, to masticate. It comes from the Hebrew thought of chewing the cud. Martin Luther said he studied his Bible as he gathered apples. First he shook the whole tree, that the ripest might fall; then he shook each limb, and when he had shaken each limb, he shook each branch, and after each branch, each twig; and then he looked under every leaf. The implication is to search the Bible as a whole, shaking the whole tree. Read it rapidly, as you would any other book. Then shake every limb—study book after book. Then shake every branch, giving attention to the chapters when they do not break the sense. Then shake each twig, by a careful study of the paragraphs and sentences. And you will be rewarded if you will look under each leaf, by searching the meaning of the words.[8]

If there is anything I commend to you it is to take this Book and to live with it; to live it, to learn it, to search it, to meditate on it, and let it become the very meat and drink of your soul. This is how our Saviour lived; this is how Joshua lived; and it is how we must live.

God's foremost command to Joshua was to *live* this Book of the Law and to obey whatever God had revealed to His servant, Moses. The Word was to become so ingrained in him, so integral a part of his thinking that his natural bent was to live the Book. The same holds true for us. That demands much more than a quiet time of five minutes in the morning with a hurried prayer before rushing off to work. It requires that you grapple with this Book before your newspaper, before your fiction, before your television, until it becomes your meat and drink; until it causes you to stretch—to stand on tiptoe to be all that the Word requires. Only when God finds a nucleus of people in this country who are ready to live the Bible, will He pour out the revival that will turn our land from defeat to victory.

Think of Britain in one of the darkest hours of her history. There seemed to be little hope of deliverance or blessing. Then God raised up John Wesley to speak to the nation. Riding across the land on horseback, with a Bible in his hand and the Holy Spirit in his heart, he brought England to repentance. In the language of the historian, J. R. Green, "The temper of the English people was changed overnight." Like Joshua, John Wesley wholly trusted the Lord.

What God did with these men He can do with our lives if we are prepared to trust His purpose, His promise, and His power. May we with sincerity pray this prayer together:

> Father . . . there may be times when I shall not be able to sense Your presence or to be aware of Your

nearness. When I am lonely and by myself, I trust You to be my companion. When I am tempted to sin, I trust You to keep me from it. When I am depressed and anxious, I trust You to lift my spirits. When I am crushed by responsibility and overwhelmed by the demands of people on my time, I trust You to give me poise and a sense of purpose. When I am rushed and running, I trust You to make me still inside. When I forget You, I trust that You will never forget me. When I forget others, I trust You to prompt me to think of them. When You take something or someone from me that I want to keep, when You remove the props I lean on for comfort in place of You; when You refuse to respond to my questions and to answer my too-selfish prayers, I will trust You even then. Amen.[9]

# Joshua 3:1-7

Then Joshua rose early in the morning; and they set out from Acacia Grove and came to the Jordan, he and all the Children of Israel, and lodged there before they crossed over.

So it was, after three days, that the officers went through the camp; and they commanded the people, saying, "When you see the ark of the covenant of the Lord your God, and the priests, the Levites, bearing it, then you shall set out from your place and go after it.

"Yet there shall be a space between you and it, about two thousand cubits by measure. Do not come near it, that you may know the way by which you must go, for you have not passed this way before."

And Joshua said to the people, "Sanctify yourselves, for tomorrow the Lord will do wonders among you."

Then Joshua spoke to the priests, saying, "Take up the ark of the covenant and cross over before the people." So they took up the ark of the covenant and went before the people.

And the Lord said to Joshua, "This day I will begin to magnify you in the sight of all Israel, that they may know that, as I was with Moses, so I will be with you."

# 8
## THE PLACE OF
# LIVING

Forty years of wandering in the wilderness are over. A new generation has emerged; a new tomorrow is on the horizon. Joshua, chosen by God and selected by Moses is about to lead 2½ million people into Canaan. Standing on the edge of the Jordan, Joshua reminds the Children of Israel that they have not passed this way before. The man of faith gives these instructions: "Sanctify yourselves, for tomorrow the Lord will do wonders among you" (Josh. 3:5). Then Joshua spoke to the priests, saying, "Take up the ark of the covenant and cross over before the people" (v. 6). And they took up the ark of the covenant and went before the people.

Have you come to your Jordan? Do you wonder what is beyond those dark waters, what lies ahead in that distant future? You have heard about it; perhaps God has given you premonitions of the fullness of blessing that there is in Himself, but you have not stepped into His purpose; you are still floundering and frightened on the banks of Jordan. I want to say to you, "Sanctify yourselves, for tomorrow the Lord will do wonders among you . . . . Take up the ark of the covenant and cross over" (vv. 5-6).

## Spiritual Preparation

The place of living calls first of all, for spiritual preparation. The first time we find the word *sanctify* is in Genesis 2:3 where "God blessed the seventh day and sanctified it" as a day of rest. Later, He amplified that to show that it was the day of worship and service to God. So the first mention of the term sanctify is exactly the same word that Joshua uses here.

Tomorrow is foreboding; tomorrow is frightening, unless you know what it is to be prepared. But what does that mean? Sanctification, as far as the Bible is concerned, means precisely two things expounded for us in the last message that Joshua gave to his people: "And if it seems evil to you to serve the Lord, choose for yourselves this day whom you will serve . . . . But as for me and my house, we will serve the Lord . . . . You cannot serve the Lord, for He is a holy God. He is a jealous God; He will not forgive your transgressions nor your sins" (Josh. 24:15, 19).

To be in the place of living, you must know separation from sin. I fear for anyone who dares to step into the unknown without the forgiveness of God. Jesus died to deal with the guilt of sin, the power of sin and one day, the very presence of sin in your life. Dr. Clarence Macartney tells of Copernicus, the great Polish mathematician whose studies and calculations revolutionized the thoughts of mankind about the universe: When he lay dying, his book which had just been printed, *The Revolution of the Heavenly Bodies,* was laid in his arms. Yet this great intellect who told the number of the stars and pronounced the laws of the universe, in the presence of God, saw himself not as the scholar or astronomer, but only as a sinner. On his grave today at Frauenberg, can be read these words: "I do not seek a kindness equal to that given Paul, nor do I ask the grace granted Peter. But that forgiveness which Thou didst grant to the robber—that, earnestly, I crave."[1]

That forgiveness, thank God, is available to the repentant sinner. John writes, "The blood of Jesus Christ His Son cleanses us from all sin" (1 John 1:7) and the writer to the Hebrews talks about being sanctified by the blood of Jesus (Heb. 10:29).

But sanctification is not only separation from sin, it is dedication for service. Every single Israelite was told to sanctify himself, for Canaan was going to represent fellowship with God, as well as service for God. It would involve soldiering—beating down the cities of the Canaanites, carving out a new land, planting vineyards, entering into the possessions that God had purposed for His people. This called for total dedication. One of the first men to dedicate himself was Joshua, when he knelt before the Man with a drawn sword, took the shoes from his feet and owned Him as the Lord of Hosts (Josh. 5:14-15).

Such a declaration is costly. On December 8, 1934 Betty Scott Stam and her husband calmly and bravely laid down their lives for Christ when they were martyred by Chinese Communists. Nine years earlier Betty had written a covenant of consecration: "Lord, I give up my own purposes and plans, all my own desires and hopes and ambitions (whether they be fleshly or soulish), and accept Thy will for my life. I give myself, my life, my all utterly to Thee, to be Thine for ever. I hand over to Thy keeping all of my friendships; all the people I love are to take a second place in my heart. Fill me and seal me with Thy Holy Spirit. Work out Thy whole will in my life, at any cost, now and forever. To me to live is Christ. Amen!"

I am inviting you to sanctify yourself by coming to the Cross in repentance and faith, and then by looking up to the throne and yielding your life—spirit, soul, and body—in complete dedication. I must say I don't promise you any hope, any joy, any victory, any life tomorrow unless you are prepared.

## Personal Expectation

The place of living calls for personal expectation. Isn't it thrilling to know that we can face tomorrow with liberated attitudes; that for the child of God there is nothing to fear. God means what He says when He affirms, "I will do wonders among you," and all that happened in past years is just a glimpse of what He wants to do, because "every day with Jesus is sweeter than the day before."

What were those wonders? Obviously, the first one in this context was the miraculous crossing of Jordan. Let us remember that in Joshua's time they did not have the means of fording rivers that we have today. Jordan presented a threatening barrier. As a matter of fact, it was floodtime so there was the added danger that the Jordan would overflow its banks. Turn to Jeremiah 12:5 and look at a verse that is extremely interesting in relation to the flooding of Jordan: "If you have run with the footmen, and they have wearied you, then how can you contend with horses? And if in the land of peace, in which you trusted, they wearied you, then how will you do in the flooding of Jordan?" And in Jeremiah 49:19 there is another reference to the swelling of Jordan. Historians and Bible scholars tell us that at a certain spot in Jordan, just about this very point, there was a great area of wildlife, filled particularly with lions. When the river overflowed at harvest time this area was completely inundated. The lions would leave the forest around that part of Jordan and prowl all over the area, both in Canaan and the other side of the bank. So with floodtide and lions, it was quite a hazard for the Children of Israel.

I have always accepted Jordan as a type of death. It was the river into which our Lord stepped in order to identify Himself with His passion ministry. He went down into the waters; He was buried in the waters; He rose up from the waters. It speaks of the river of death.

There is only one answer to sin, self, and Satan: it is the death on the cross. If the lions speak of Satan, the people in their own fearfulness speak of the flesh, and their hearts of sin speak of that which always haunts the believing soul, then death in Jordan is the only answer. However, *they* were afraid to accept that death because they did not know the secret; yet God said, "Sanctify yourselves, for tomorrow the Lord will do wonders among you" (Josh. 3:5).

To one who asked him the secret of his service, George Mueller said: "There was a day when I died, *utterly died,*" and, as he spoke, he bent lower and lower until he almost touched the floor. "Died to George Mueller, his opinions, preferences, tastes, and will—died to the world, its approval or censure—died to the approval or blame even of my brethren and friends—and since then I have studied only to show myself approved unto God."[3] Such faith as demonstrated by Mueller and others unlocks the secret of miraculously crossing Jordan. Many times you are going to face sin, self, and Satan. But each time you can cross Jordan by faith as you claim the victory through our Lord Jesus Christ.

Many people have tried to live the victorious Christian life through their own efforts. Perhaps you have too. Such persons are missing the mark. They have misunderstood what it means to be in right relationship with the Father. As Dr. Shoemaker explains, "There is the great relationship between God and those who honestly love and seek His will. There is a Person at the heart of things. We can talk with Him and cooperate and plan and rejoice and be serious, just as we can with the person closest in all the world to us. God is not that kind of person to many, and for good reason—they have wanted other things more than Him, or refused to surrender something He wants them to surrender, or never taken time enough to be really with Him in prayer. Vaguely some of us believe in

Him, but we have not found Him. But you can find Him. He is there to be found. And when you find Him, you will find joy with Him, such joy as you never knew without Him."[4] He is speaking of the kind of relationship that allows the Spirit to flow in and through us, enabling us to consistently overcome Satan's attacks.

The second wonder was the victorious conquest of Canaan. "By this you shall know that the living God is among you, and that He will without fail drive out from before you the Canaanites and the Hittites and the Hivites and the Perizzites and the Girgashites and the Amorites and the Jebusites" (Josh. 3:10). I interpret this verse in terms of Ephesians 6. If self, sin, and Satan represent the attacks on an earthly level, then these seven nations of Canaan represent the battle which is being waged in heavenly places. "For we do not wrestle against flesh and blood, but against principalities, against powers, against the rulers of the darkness of this age, against spiritual hosts of wickedness in the heavenly places" (Eph. 6:12).

What is happening in the Middle East, in Africa, and in other war-ravaged areas is only the "rulers of the darkness of this age" manipulating flesh and blood to fulfill their purpose in heavenly places. Bombs and bullets can never deal with that. Only faith in a mighty God can assure us of victory.

But be encouraged! "We are a supernatural people, born again by a supernatural birth; we wage a supernatural fight and are taught by a supernatural teacher, led by a supernatural captain to assured victory."[5] The promise was that "tomorrow the Lord will do wonders among you" (Josh. 3:5). And so it happened. The first thing that met the Children of Israel on the other side of Jordan was the high walls of Jericho. How was that city to be razed? A contemporary of Martin Luther said, "The whole world is against you, Martin." The intrepid reformer said, "Then it is God and Luther against the whole world."[6] As Joshua faced a myriad of obstacles in Canaan, he could well have said, "It is God and Joshua against the whole of Canaan!" Those walls were formidable. How were they to meet the challenge? By blowing rams' horns and marching around those walls in faith seven times—every day once, and on the seventh day seven times in order that they might realize the enormity of this great barrier and understand their total helplessness to do anything within their own power. Joshua and his army were obedient. Jericho crumbled. After they had learned their lesson, Ai went down and every single nation in Canaan until each of the seven nations was subdued.

## Actual Realization

The place of living calls for spiritual preparation, for personal expectation, and for actual realization. Note that in Joshua 3 there are no less than 10 mentions of the ark. That chest, covered within and without with gold, with the mercy seat on top of it, was a symbol of the presence of God amid His people throughout all their wanderings. Within that ark were the tables of stone, speaking of our searching Saviour who convicts us of our sin. There was the budding rod, which speaks of the redeeming Saviour who saves us by His life. And there was the pot of manna, speaking of the satisfying Saviour who feeds our souls.

It is important to notice that preparation and expectation never found realization until the ark was put where it belonged. The ark had to be preferred. According to our text the ark had to go first, carried by the priests, and be placed in the center of the biggest problem, which was Jordan. The moment those waters were touched by the feet of the priests the miraculous happened. The waters receded; the riverbed dried up, and the once threatening Jordan became a highway for the Children of Israel. The ark was placed at the center of that riverbed and rested there until everyone had crossed over.

The heart of the biblical message is that Jesus Christ must have unrivaled first place in your life. "For to this end Christ died and rose and lived again, that He might be Lord" (Rom. 14:9). We cannot control our lives while we claim that Christ is Lord. Again, it is Dr. Shoemaker who gets to the point with laser-beam penetration: "We only really know God as He manifested Himself in Christ. Sometimes we get impatient. Having ignored God while the sun was shining, we come running to Him when the clouds gather saying, 'What shall I do?' I think He says something like this: 'Get quiet for a while. You have been feverishly pursuing your own will for a long time. Before I can tell you what to do, you must let Me come into your life, not just for occasional help, but for good and all. Do you really want to know My will, and do it, or do you want Me to sanction your will, and help you get what you want?' . . . We shall find that we can't seek the will of God in some areas, but only in all."[7]

That's the key to living under the Lordship of Christ—seeking Him in all things, because God has decreed that in the universe, in creation, in the church, in the Christian life, Christ must have the preeminence. If tomorrow is going to be the day of wonders for you, then Christ must be preferred in your life. Just as there was a spot in the Jordan River where the ark had to rest, so Christ must rest in the place that He demands in our lives. It might be the very place that threatens and frightens us, but there the Lord must come and rest.

Let John the Baptist be our example. Concerning Jesus, John said, "After me comes a Man who is preferred before me, for He was before me" (John 1:30). Again, he said, "He must increase, but I must decrease" (3:30).

The ark had to be perceived. That was a strategic move of God through Joshua to the people so that the ark was never obscured. If the Children of Israel had followed directly behind the priests they would never have seen the ark because of the mass of people; but so long as they were at least half a mile removed they could see the ark being carried to the river and resting there. Keeping the ark in view was their only hope of realizing the wonders of God.

It is one thing to make Christ Lord of your life; it is another thing to keep your eyes on Him moment by moment. Hundreds of times we have seen individuals stand to their feet to yield their lives to the Lordship of Christ, but within a week's time they have collapsed in total defeat, simply because they failed to keep their eyes on Jesus.

No story in the New Testament illustrates this principle so dramatically and helpfully as the account of Peter walking on the water. Remember how the Saviour called him? When Peter recognized that it was the Lord Himself, he stepped out of the boat. As long as his eyes were focused on Christ, he became the master of the wind and the waves and actually walked on the water. But when in a moment of doubt he took his eyes off the Master, he began to sink and had to cry, "Lord, save me!" And Jesus was there to save him. But notice the Lord's question: "O you of little faith, why did you doubt?" (See Matt. 14:26-31.)

Every time a Christian takes his eyes off the Lord Jesus Christ and loses the vision of the Saviour, he will fail miserably. There is no better way to keep our eyes on the Lord Jesus than to have our daily quiet time—to read the Word, to spend time in prayer, and to seek the fullness of the Holy Spirit. Never have a day without meeting your Saviour; always submit to the empowering presence of the Holy Spirit.

The ark had to be preferred; the ark had to be perceived; and finally, the ark had to be pursued. In our language this is simply a directive to follow Him. It is the message of discipleship. "If anyone desires to come after Me, let him deny himself, and take up his cross, and follow Me" (Matt. 16:24). God is ever moving and we must follow Him. And as you go after God He will not only lead you through Jericho, through Ai, but throughout the whole length and breadth of Canaan, for He wants you to put your foot down on every part of that land and possess your possession. "Eye has not seen, nor ear heard, nor have entered into the heart of man the things which God has prepared for those who love Him" (1 Cor. 2:9).

You may ask, how can the place of living be realized in my life? The answer is to prefer Christ, perceive Christ, and pursue Christ. If this is your aim, you will find "Canaan" a realization in your life. Crown Jesus Lord of your life. Never let Him be out of your spiritual sight. Renew that determination day by day through the Word and by the Holy Spirit. Make your daily prayer:

O Jesus, Lord and Saviour,
I give myself to Thee;
For Thou, in Thy atonement,
Didst give Thyself for me;
I own no other Master,
My heart shall be Thy throne;
My life I give, henceforth to live,
O Christ, for Thee alone.[8]

# Joshua 14:6-15; 15:13-14

Then the children of Judah came to Joshua in Gilgal. And Caleb, the son of Jephunneh the Kenizzite, said to him: "You know the word which the Lord said to Moses the man of God concerning you and me in Kadesh Barnea.

"I was forty years old when Moses, the servant of the Lord, sent me from Kadesh Barnea to spy out the land, and I brought back word to him as it was in my heart. Nevertheless my brethren who went up with me made the heart of the people melt, but I wholly followed the Lord my God.

"So Moses swore on that day, saying, 'Surely the land where your foot has trodden shall be your inheritance and your children's forever, because you have wholly followed the Lord my God.'

"And now, behold, the Lord has kept me alive, as He said, these forty-five years, ever since the Lord spoke this word to Moses while Israel wandered in the wilderness; and now, here I am this day, eighty-five years old. As yet I am as strong this day as I was on the day that Moses sent me; just as my strength was then, so now is my strength for war, both for going out and for coming in.

"Now therefore, give me this mountain of which the Lord spoke in that day; for you heard in that day how the Anakim were there, and that the cities were great and fortified. It may be that the Lord will be with me, and I shall be able to drive them out as the Lord said."

And Joshua blessed him, and gave Hebron to Caleb the son of Jephunneh as an inheritance. Hebron therefore became the inheritance of Caleb, the son of Jephunneh the Kenizzite, to this day, because he wholly followed the Lord God of Israel. And the name of Hebron formerly was Kirjath Arba, for Arba was the greatest man among the Anakim. Then the land had rest from war.

Now to Caleb the son of Jephunneh he gave a portion among the children of Judah, according to the commandment of the Lord to Joshua, namely, Kirjath Arba, which is Hebron (Arba was the father of Anak). Caleb drove out the three sons of Anak from there: Sheshai, Ahiman, and Talmai, the children of Anak.

# 9

## THE PLACE OF

# *YIELDING*

We have seen how God has used various individuals to lead the Children of Israel out of bondage in Egypt into the fullness of blessing in Canaan. We have noted how God raised up Moses to be the deliverer of His people, then Joshua, and now another man, Caleb, enters the scene. It was Caleb, who "wholly followed the Lord" (Josh. 14:14), whose faith God honored by bringing him into the Promised Land.

Caleb was a foreigner by birth. His father, Jephunneh the Kenizzite, was outside the boundaries of the chosen people. But though disadvantaged by nativity, he "broke his birth's invidious bar" and achieved greatly. He became possessor of "another spirit" (Num. 14:24) and was thereafter counted among the people of God.

Is that the story of your life? Do you know what it is to have received God's Spirit of adoption whereby you cry, "I am my Father's now, and no longer a stranger and a foreigner, but a fellow citizen with the saints"? (See Eph. 2:19.) Until you can honestly use this language you cannot follow the deeper lessons that are to be learned from this illustrious patriot and saint of ancient Israel.

Given this "new spirit," Caleb despised the halfheartedness of men who vacillate on the periphery of God's great purpose for their lives. He was having all God's best or nothing at all. No wonder he earned the name Caleb, which means *all heart*. Caleb wholly followed the Lord his God. It cost him everything, but such wholehearted following also paid him everything.

## The Experience of a Spared Life

None can follow the Lord wholeheartedly without knowing the experience of a spared life. Caleb affirmed that the Lord had kept him alive. In other words, his life was spared from discouragement. Unlike the rest of the camp who were discouraged and murmured against God, Caleb and Joshua were spared discouragement because they wholly followed the Lord. "Caleb quieted the people" (Num. 13:30).

Men who can calm others are beyond price in our churches, businesses, and homes today. It is a task that angels might worthily covet. But it is the secret only of those who know wholehearted surrender to God—surrender evidenced by complete trust. With total commitment comes relinquishment of the control centers of our lives. We understand the merit of allowing His plan to unfold. "Wisely enough, God does not let us skip ahead in the story of our lives, but rather leads us page by page to its understandable conclusion in Him. And so, as each of us faces an uncertain future, we can trust in God's promise as expressed by Jeremiah, 'For I know the plans I have for you,' saith the Lord. 'They are plans for good and not for evil, to give a future and a hope.'"[1] (See Jer. 29:11.)

Caleb was spared from disbelief as well. Concerning the rest of the Children of Israel, "they could not enter in (i.e. into the land of promise) because of unbelief" (Heb. 3:19). But here is a man whose faith laughs at impossibilities and proclaims, "It shall be done!" Listen to his language: "Let us go up at once,

and take possession, for we are well able to overcome it"
(Num. 13:30). As Dr. Eadie puts it, "Caleb was brave among
cowards, assured among skeptics."

Nothing slays unbelief in our hearts like wholehearted surrender—that determination to go through with God, whatever
the circumstances.

> Oh for a faith that will be strong
> When angry foes beset,
> A faith that will stand fast until
> The victory is met.
>
> Though dark and long the battle rage,
> I pray for faith sincere,
> A faith that will stand out, unmoved,
> A strength in time of fear.
>
> A courage born of trust alone,
> I know will see me through;
> So, Lord, I pray, Thou mayest now
> My feeble faith renew.[2]

Caleb was spared from death. Moses died. All older Israel,
with the exception of Joshua and Caleb, died. The New Testament confirms this (Heb. 3:17). Paul, in referring to this same
fact writes, "Now all these things happened to them as examples, and they were written for our admonition, on whom the
ends of the ages have come (1 Cor. 10:11).

This principle of death is still at work today. Paul warns, "For
if you live according to flesh, you will die" (Rom. 8:13); "the
wages of sin is death" (6:23); "for this reason many are weak
and sick among you, and many sleep" (1 Cor. 11:30). John
also declares, "All unrighteousness is sin, and there is sin not

leading to death" (1 John 5:17). The Lord Jesus suggests the same solemn truth when He says, "Every branch in Me that does not bear fruit He takes away" (John 15:2).

Death, for the believer, can never mean spiritual death, but it may and does mean spiritual barrenness or physical death, as past and contemporary history well illustrate. But why die in this way? Caleb says that the Lord kept him alive! When Martin Luther was in the throes of the Reformation and the Pope was trying to bring him back to the Catholic Church, he sent a cardinal to deal with Luther and buy him with gold. The cardinal wrote to the Pope, "The fool does not love gold." The cardinal, when he could not convince Luther, said to him, "What do you think the Pope cares for the opinion of a German boor? The Pope s little finger is stronger than all Germany. Do you expect your princes to take up arms to defend you—you, a wretched worm like you? I tell you, *No.* And where will you be then?" Luther's reply was simple: "Where I am now. In the hands of the Almighty God."[3] Caleb, though he faced opposition of various kinds, was kept from death by the power of the Almighty God.

## The Experience of a Strong Life

Issuing from a surrendered life is the experience of a strong life. At 85 years of age, Caleb was strong enough for victorious warfare. He could *go out* and *come in.* Indeed, in Joshua 15:14 we read: "Caleb drove out the three sons of Anak." Anak, whose name means giant or long-necked, was the son of Arba. His name signifies *the strength of Baal.* In New Testament language, Anak corresponds to all that is in the world which is not of God; in other words, the trinity of evil which John describes as "the lust of the flesh, the lust of the eyes, and pride of life" (1 John 2:16). Examine carefully these three aspects representing the forces of temptation which were employed by the devil to seduce Eve in the Garden and the Lord Jesus in the wilderness. Here, then, are three giants with whom every true Christian is confronted.

There is the giant of lustful passions—"the lust of the flesh." The word lust signifies a strong desire, while the flesh stands for that carnal nature of fallen man which uses the body as its instrument. The flesh is therefore, the seat of sin in man. Uncontrolled passions are the cause of every form of perversion in human life. Talk about moral delinquency in the past has been cheap. In some instances, the subject has been the hobbyhorse of the alarmists. The time has come, however, when the matter can no longer be ignored. Responsible people throughout the world are confessing that the problem is no longer just pitiful and deserving of our sympathy and resource, but it is, when multiplied, a threat to our social order. Because of uncontrolled passions, individual lives are ruined, homes are wrecked, and society is corrupted. The alarming thing about it is that such lustful perversions are making tremendous inroads into our church life. This first son of Anak is having his way in religious circles as perhaps never before. Caleb knew how to drive him out. Are you conquering him, or are you a slave to uncontrolled passions?

Second, there is the giant of lustful pleasures—"the lust of the eyes." This is a special form of gratification. The desire may be for the artistic and aesthetic, which though in itself is beautiful, may so engage the heart as to hinder fellowship with God. The world has gone mad over pleasures of one kind and another. Some have stated that pleasure has become one of our major national liabilities. People are living for the present and grasping at what they can see. They have lost all hold on what is unseen and spiritual.

Here again, the church has suffered. In fact, in many instances she has succumbed to the very same thing. The believer has to learn to say, "Turn away my eyes from looking at worthless things" (Ps. 119:37).

There is a sobering story of a famous blacksmith of medieval times who, having been taken a prisoner and cast into a dungeon, began to examine the chain that bound him, with a view to discovering some flaw that might make it easier to be broken. His hope was in vain, for he found from marks on it, that it was of his own workmanship, and it had been his boast that none could break a chain that he had forged. Lustful pleasures are like those chains. We forge them ourselves and when we wish to be free, we discover that they cannot be broken. Only the power of God can keep us free from the tyranny of lustful pleasures.[4]

Because he wholly followed the Lord, Caleb was equal even to this son of Anak—lustful pleasures. We need to give serious thought to our own positions. Are we conquerors or have we been pulled into this fatal vortex of worldly pleasure and lustful materialism?

Third, there is the giant of lustful power—"the pride of life" or "the vainglory of life." Lord Acton once said, "Power tends to corrupt; absolute power tends to corrupt absolutely." Man is essentially an exhibitionist because of his inherent conceit and arrogance. Perhaps this is why John uses a word which the early Greeks employed to describe a proud or vainglorious man. Literally, it is a term which might be rendered a boaster or a braggart. For this reason people will grasp at riches in order to become financially powerful; they will seize on status in order to become socially powerful; they will inculcate knowledge in order to be intellectually powerful.

The tragedy is that this spirit of vainglory has entered our church life; even within religious ranks man is out for power. Oh, the pride, the jealousy, and cruelty of worldly prominence! A chairman, introducing Dr. Jonathan Goforth to a Chicago audience, spoke glowingly of him as a brilliant speaker and as a missionary who had accomplished great things. In acknowledging the words of praise, Dr. Goforth said, "When I listen to such words of adulation, I am reminded of the story of a proud woodpecker that lighted on a tall dead pine tree and began to peck. Just then a bolt of lightening struck the dead tree and splintered it into smithereens! The terror-strickened bird flew and lighted on a nearby tree. Regaining its composure, it looked down at the splinter heap and proudly exclaimed, 'Look what I did!' Too many of God's men fall prey to the giant of lustful power and imagine that they are something when they are indeed nothing."[5]

Perhaps this is the toughest of the three giants, but Caleb was more than equal to all three of them. The record shows that "Caleb drove out the three sons of Anak" (Josh. 15:14). They were great in size, but he was greater in spirit. Though they had faces like lions, they had hearts like frightened hares. Caleb overcame them by the power of a surrendered life.

The principle of true victory is just the same today. The believer who overcomes can only do so in the strength of a yielded life. The Son of God, who was manifested that He might destroy the works of the devil must have the wholehearted surrender of the would-be conquering Christian.

## The Experience of a Satisfied Life
Consider the third blessing which flowed, and flows, from a surrendered life. It is the experience of a satisfied life. "Joshua blessed him, and gave Hebron to Caleb . . . as an inheritance. . . . Then the land had rest from war" (14:13-15). In these three statements are the true ingredients of a satisfied life, one of which is spiritual prosperity. David says concerning the blessed man, "Whatever he does shall prosper" (Ps. 1:3). The sense that God is with a man, blessing his life and work, is the

first ingredient in the experience of true satisfaction. Caleb knew this experience. In his honored old age, he proclaims, "I wholly followed the Lord my God."

Scholars say that the figure of the original words is nautical. The idea is that of a ship in full sail, a vessel which goes straight on. Whether the seas were rough or smooth, God made the ship of Caleb's life to ride prosperously. Not only could Caleb give this testimony, but Moses could say of him, "You have wholly followed the Lord my God" (Josh. 14:9). Even greater still came the witness from heaven itself: "My servant Caleb . . . has followed Me fully" (Num. 14:24).

Among the Japanese horticulturists, there is a method used by which certain trees are stunted and kept small. Early in the life of the tree, the Japanese tie off the tap roots through which life must flow to the farthest branch. This keeps the tree undernourished so that is never attains the growth others of its variety reach. Failure on the part of a Christian to commit himself wholly to God shuts off the life-giving flow of divine grace, so that he denies himself the opportunity to grow to full stature in Christ.[6]

In this age of compromise, blessed are the uncompromisingly faithful ones. Well is it recorded that "Joshua blessed him" (Josh. 14:13). Do you know this spiritual prosperity?

Another ingredient of a satisfied life is in the realm of spiritual possessions. Remember that this inheritance had been Caleb's by promise for 45 years, but now he consciously possessed it. The Hebron of spiritual blessings in Christ is available only to the fully-surrendered believer. Paul says, "I beseech you . . . by the mercies of God, that you present your bodies a living sacrifice, holy, acceptable to God, which is your reasonable service. And do not be conformed to this world, but be transformed by the renewing of your mind, that you may prove what is that good and acceptable and perfect will of

God" (Rom. 12:1-2). He also reminds us that "God . . . has blessed us with every spiritual blessing in the heavenly places in Christ" (Eph. 1:3). It is ours, then, to possess our possessions in Christ by an act of appropriating faith. Our "Heavenly Joshua" has given us all things in Himself, and it is our privilege to enter into everything that Christ has purchased for us.

A man on the great Texas oil fields said, "I know the man that used to own this land. He could scarcely make a living. Speculators bought up his land for a small price. They sank oil wells, and today the land is worth millions." At one time the farmer owned every drop of that oil. But he did not possess the wealth, though all of it was his.[7] Are you enjoying your spiritual possessions in Christ?

Spiritual peace, in terms of spiritual experience, is the final evidence of a satisfied life. I do not mean to imply by this that the Christian's war ever ceases while he is on earth, but I do affirm that in answer to a full surrender, the believer may know the rest of being more than conqueror. Enemies were still around Caleb, and every now and again he had to fight them; but their presence gave him no unrest or worry. He was at rest in the fact that through God's power he was more than conqueror.

Similarly, the wholly yielded believer can know such a victory in the indwelling Christ that previous strivings and strugglings are calmed into a glorious rest of faith. The believer no longer tries in the flesh, but rather trusts in the empowering Christ to make real in and through him all that Calvary's victory means. That is why the writer to the Hebrews says, "He who has entered His rest has himself also ceased from his works as God did from His" (Heb. 4:10).

Here, then, is the threefold experience which flows from a wholehearted surrender to God in the place of yielding: a spared life, a strong life, a satisfied life. God is looking for yielded men and women today—people who are under His sparing, strengthening, and satisfying control.

I remember once hearing of a tragic train wreck. Suffering people, broken limbs, many trapped and dying—all were a part of the scene. One of the more fortunate passengers recognized a gentleman who had also apparently escaped unscathed. "Excuse me, Sir," asked the man, "But aren't you a doctor?" "Yes," replied the man. "Well," his questioner cried, "Why don't you do something? Can't you see dying people all around you?" The obviously distressed doctor made this reply: "My friend, I'm doing all I can, but I'm greatly handicapped because I have no instruments."

Today a bruised and dying world cried out to God, "Why don't you do something?" And I cannot help feeling that the reply from heaven is much the same as that of the doctor, "I would do something, but I have no instruments."

It was because Paul knew of God's need for human instruments that he pleaded, "Present yourselves to God as being alive from the dead, and *your members as instruments of righteousness to God"* (Rom. 6:13).

How we need such surrender and yieldedness today! Will you face the challenge quietly and then give your answer to God?

> In full and glad surrender,
> I give myself to Thee,
> Thine utterly and only
> And evermore to be.[8]

# Deuteronomy 11:10-21

"For the land which you go to possess is not like the land of Egypt from which you have come, where you sowed your seed and watered it by foot, as a vegetable garden; but the land which you cross over to possess is a land of hills and valleys, which drinks water from the rain of heaven, a land for which the Lord your God cares; the eyes of the Lord your God are always on it, from the beginning of the year to the very end of the year.

"And it shall be that if you diligently obey My commandments which I command you today, to love the Lord your God and serve Him with all your heart and with all your soul, then I will give you the rain for your land in its season, the early rain and the latter rain, that you may gather in your grain, your new wine, and your oil. And I will send grass in your fields for your livestock, that you may eat and be filled.

"Take heed to yourselves, lest your heart be deceived, and you turn aside and serve other gods and worship them, lest the Lord's anger be aroused against you, and He shut up the heavens so that there be no rain, and the land yield no produce, and you perish quickly from the good land which the Lord is giving you.

"Therefore you shall lay up these words of Mine in your heart and in your soul, and bind them as a sign on your hand, and they shall be as frontlets between your eyes. You shall teach them to your children, speaking of them when you sit in your house, when you walk by the way, when you lie down, and when you rise up. And you shall write them on the doorposts of your house and on your gates, that your days and the days of your children may be multiplied in the land of which the Lord swore to your fathers to give them, like the days of the heavens above the earth."

# THE PLACE OF

# *BLESSING*

God's purpose for His people is that they might be in the place of blessing in order to experience "days of heaven above the earth" (Deut. 11:21). In the Scripture under consideration we have seen how this design of love was expressed in the early prosperity which was promised to the Children of Israel and how, in this day of grace, God desires that the church should know that same experience in terms of spiritual blessing. These verses remarkably demonstrate how God's provisions and conditions of blessing may become ours.

God's abounding provisions for His children are apparent in His promise "the good land which the Lord is giving you" (v. 17). As He had promised to Abraham, Isaac, and Jacob, God had given this good land to His ancient people, the Jews. It was theirs to enter and possess. In a similar way, God has given us the good land of spiritual blessings in Christ. Writing to the Ephesians, Paul declared, "Blessed be the God and Father of our Lord Jesus Christ, who has blessed us with every spiritual blessing in the heavenly places in Christ" (Eph. 1:3).

We have no right to be spiritual paupers when God has

made us princes in Christ. The land is before us to enter and possess. We can enjoy "days of heaven upon earth" in terms of personal blessing. Let us consider some of these rewards which are ours in Christ.

## God's Abounding Provision

First is the provision of spiritual enrichment in Christ. "A land flowing with milk and honey . . . grain . . . wine . . . oil . . . livestock" (Deut. 11:9, 14-15). What was material prosperity to God's ancient people can be spiritual prosperity for us. We can know the enrichment of truth in Christ—milk, cattle, and honey. For those who are young in the faith there is "the pure milk of the Word," because Peter says, "As newborn babes, desire the pure milk of the Word, that you may grow thereby" (1 Peter 2:2). No young Christian has an excuse for retarded growth, because the milk of the Word is always available.

For those who are older in Christian experience, there is "the strong meat." God says, "I will send grass in your fields for your livestock that you may eat and be filled" (Deut. 11:15). The writer to the Hebrews reminds us that "solid food belongs to those who are of full age, that is, those who by reason of use have their senses exercised to discern both good and evil" (Heb. 5:14). There is no stage of development in Christian experience for which there is not adequate solid food.

If milk is for the young and solid food for the older, then honey is for everyone. David tells us that the Word of God is "sweeter also than honey and the honeycomb" (Ps. 19:10). And in another place he exclaims, "How sweet are Your words to my taste, sweeter than honey to my mouth" (119:103). And Jeremiah could say, "Your words were found, and I ate them; and Your Word was to me the joy and rejoicing of my heart" (Jer. 15:16).

God never commands His children to do the impossible,

but provides for their needs along the way; He gives strength for every task. The first American woman to find great success in newspaper journalism was Nellie Bly. One day as Nellie came to her desk she found an assignment that was staggering. She was to board a ship that day embarking on an around-the-world trip that was to set a new world's record. She had little money with her and no time to make necessary arrangements. Her chief told Nellie that all provisions had already been made for the trip. She left knowing that all the resources of a great metropolitan newspaper were backing her. The trip was made in record time, making headlines in newspapers around the world. Nellie Bly experienced no lack of provisions during the entire journey. In like manner, God has made previous provision for those embarking on the Christian life including the power to live victoriously.[1] Here then, is the enrichment of truth in Christ.

Second is the enrichment of life in Christ. Canaan is a land of grain. Jesus reminds us, "Most assuredly, I say to you, unless a grain of wheat falls into the ground and dies, it remains alone; but if it dies, it produces much grain" (John 12:24). Willingness to die with Christ is rewarded by resurrection life in all its fullness. Paul has the same thought when he says: "The law of the Spirit of life in Christ Jesus has made me free from the law of sin and death" (Rom. 8:2). This is the abundant life which Jesus came to give us. Do you know anything of the grain of Canaan?

Dr. Howard M. Kelly found the secret of enrichment and expresses it in these words: "My own daily life is as full as that of any man I know, but I found long since that as I allowed the pressure of professional and other engagements to fill in every moment between rising and going to bed, the spirit would surely starve. I made a rule, which I have since stuck to in spite of many temptations, not to read or study anything but my

Bible after the evening meal, and never to read any other book but the Bible on Sunday."[2]

Third is the enrichment of joy in Christ, for this is a land of wine. We are told that wine gladdens the heart of man. No wonder the outside world accused the disciples on the Day of Pentecost of being "full of new wine" (Acts 2:13). The fact of the matter was that they were filled with the Holy Spirit. The Bible tells us that "the fruit of the Spirit is . . . joy" (Gal. 5:22) and that "the kingdom of God is not food and drink, but righteousness and peace and joy in the Holy Spirit" (Rom. 14:17). Years ago, a Boston newspaper commented on the weather in this manner: "The day opened cloudy and cheerless but about noon Phillips Brooks came downtown and everything brightened up." What a marvelous tribute! What an example of an outward expression of inward joy!

As we go further in the text, we notice that fourth comes the enrichment of power in Christ inasmuch as Canaan is the land of oil. Power is symbolized in the Scriptures by the oil of anointing. The Lord Jesus undoubtedly had this in mind when He said, "You shall receive power when the Holy Spirit has come upon you" (Acts 1:8). This is both the power to appreciate truth as well as to communicate truth. John says, "You have an anointing from the Holy One, and you know all things" (1 John 2:20). And Paul reminds us that the authority to be able to say the *yes* of truth and mean it comes from God. "He who establishes us with you in Christ and has anointed us is God, who also has sealed us and given us the Spirit in our hearts" (2 Cor. 1:21-22).

According to R. A. Torrey, the secret of D. L. Moody's success was found in Psalm 62:11: "God has spoken once, twice I have heard this: That power belongs to God." Torrey continues: "I am glad it does. I am glad that power did not belong to D. L. Moody; I am glad that it did not belong to Charles G.

Finney; I am glad that it did not belong to Martin Luther; I am glad that it did not belong to any other Christian . . . in this world's history. Power belongs to God."[3] And we might add that with God there is never a power shortage!

In God's wisdom, He provides spiritual refreshment in Christ. To show the uniqueness of this heavenly refreshment, the inspired writer reminds the Children of Israel that the irrigation of Egypt involved both human activity and human anxiety. "For the land which you go to possess is not like the land of Egypt from which you have come, where you sowed your seed and watered it by foot, as a vegetable garden" (Deut. 11:10). Egypt was dependent upon the floodtides of the river Nile. If the river failed to rise, there was no water and therefore, no crops. And even when there was sufficient water, it had to be channeled through the gardens by digging ditches with the feet. How descriptive of the feverish activity and anxiety of the natural man—and of the carnal man as well.

In Canaan, however, "the rain of heaven" was promised in abundance, whether on the hill or in the valley. How precious to know that whether in the place of exaltation or even in the place of humiliation, God has promised to reach us with His water from heaven! The hills may speak of our capacity to believe, as we ascend in prayer and faith, whereas the valleys signify our capacity to receive, as we humble ourselves in repentance and brokenness. Whatever it is, God has promised to send rain in due season. So it is that when we need spiritual refreshment it is available in Christ.

We must not fail to notice that there is the provision of spiritual contentment in Christ. "A land for which the Lord your God cares; the eyes of the Lord your God are always on it, from the beginning of the year to the very end of the year" (Deut. 11:12). These matchless words describe the life of contentment—a contentment embodied in the person of Fanny

Crosby. Even though she lost her sight as a child, Fanny Crosby was not discouraged. Out of her misfortune came scores of the sweetest songs of the church. Physically handicapped herself, the contentment of Christ prompted her to write:

> Oh, what a happy soul am I!
> Although I cannot see,
> I am resolved that in this world
> Contented I will be.
> How many blessings I enjoy
> That other people don't!
> To weep and sigh because I'm blind
> I cannot and I won't![4]

Such contentment comes from an understanding that God's children are ever under His watchful care. We are speaking of a life of unbroken fellowship with the Eternal. When Solomon finished building the temple, God appeared to him and said, "I have sanctified this house which you have built to put My name there forever, and My eyes and My heart will be there perpetually" (1 Kings 9:3).

This idea of being under the eyes of God is very significant in the Holy Scriptures. Three different words are employed in the Old Testament to describe the believer as the apple of God's eye. The first one is translated *little man;* the second, *daughter;* the third, *the pupil of the eye.* Just as a small boy has to be protected from the bully, and just as a godly father jealously shields his virgin daughter; just as the pupil of the eye is guarded by the sensitive and accurate mechanism of the eyelid, so God takes care of His own. "A land for which the Lord your God cares; the eyes of the Lord your God are always on it, from the beginning of the year to the very end of the year" (Deut. 11:12). Given here is a word picture of the presence and peacefulness of contentment! God has invaded this world in the person of the Lord Jesus Christ in order to give us spiritual enrichment, refreshment, and contentment. These are God's provisions for His children.

## God's Abiding Condition

But now we must consider the second truth which is laid down for us in these verses which are God's abiding conditions for His children. With all the provisions that are available for the child of God, it is characteristic of the typical Christian to be poverty-stricken and spiritually defeated. The reason is simply that he has not gone into the land to make it his very own. God has provisions for His children, but He also has conditions; they are set out for us in no uncertain language. Observe, first of all, the directive conditions. "And it shall be that if you diligently obey My commandments which I command you today, to love the Lord your God and serve Him with all your heart and with all your soul" (Deut. 11:13). In a sentence, this condition calls for a hearing, loving, and serving obedience to Almighty God.

James T. White has said that perhaps the most effective illustration of obedience is the reply of the mother of George Washington made at the banquet given to the allied officers after the surrender of Lord Cornwallis. A distinguished French officer asked Washington's mother how she had managed to rear such a splendid son. She replied, "I taught him to obey."[5] God teaches all His children to obey, for obedience is the condition of blessing. Such obedience will be evident in our personal, social, and vocational lives.

God so impressed upon His people the need for obedience that the Hebrew people symbolized this obedience by putting excerpts of the Law in little wooden or metal containers, which were secured to the hand, or bound as frontlets between the eyes. This is not what God intended. True obedience is a matter of the heart and of the soul and of daily behavior.

Paul may well have been thinking of these words in Deuteronomy when he exhorted all men everywhere to pray, lifting up holy hands (1 Tim. 2:8). Only a person who prays like this can live obediently in his personal life.

There must be total obedience to God in our social life. True obedience to God will affect everything to do with our homes; our spouse and children will be sanctified by such living; the Word of God will be the subject of discussion when we sit down; it will dominate our thoughts as we walk, or as we lie down, and when we rise early in the morning. The whole of our social life will feel the impact of our true obedience to God.

There must be total obedience to God in our vocational life. "Aboard a man-of-war," revealed an old sailor, "there's only two things—duty or mutiny." It is precisely the same in the Christian life—either it is duty—obeying the Lord, or mutiny—disobeying His Word and His will.[6] No one can leave his home for daily work without being reminded of the demands of the Word of God, if they are secured to the doorpost of the house. And even in the gates of the city, God's name will be honored, and His commandments obeyed.

In the early days, business transactions and governmental rulings were made at the gates of the city. In other words, these gates symbolized all that constituted the daily round and common task; but right in this area of life the will of God was to be done on earth as it was in heaven. Only then would the Children of Israel know "the days of the heavens above the earth" (Deut. 11:21).

And the same is true today. We can talk endlessly about the abounding provisions of God, but unless we go in to possess them by fulfilling the conditions which God has laid down, we can be even more miserable than the unregenerate around us. Let us remember what these directive conditions involve: obedience in loving, hearing, and serving God until the effect is seen in our personal, social, and vocational lives.

## God's Attending Benediction

Knowing the human heart, God has given us not only directive conditions, but also the corrective conditions. "Take heed to yourselves, lest your heart be deceived, and you turn aside and serve other gods and worship them, lest the Lord's anger be aroused against you, and He shut up the heavens so that there be no rain, and the land yield no produce, and you perish quickly from the good land which the Lord is giving you" (Deut. 11:16-17).

These solemn words are a warning to all who fail to go in and possess the land which the Lord has given to His people. They describe the four steps that lead to God's judgment on His people. There is, first of all, a deceitfulness of heart. The Bible tells us that "the heart is deceitful above all things and desperately wicked" (Jer. 17:9). John confirms this by writing that "if we say that we have no sin, we deceive ourselves, and the truth is not in us" (1 John 1:8). Though we have received the new nature through faith in Jesus Christ, we are still possessed of that old, perverse nature which will remain until the redemption of our bodies. Unless that old nature is kept in the place of death, by the operation of the Spirit, we can be deceived into thinking that *our* way is better than God's will.

This, in turn, leads to a disobedience of heart. Disobedience, of course, is the opposite of that which we have been considering in terms of God's directive condition. It was through disobedience that Adam lost the paradise of God. It is through disobedience that we can lose the provisions of God. Cost what it will we must ever remember that "to obey is better than sacrifice" (1 Sam. 15:22).

But if we persist in disobedience, we find ourselves with a debasement of heart. Paul describes this condition when he speaks of people who change the truth of God into a lie, and worship and serve the creature more than the Creator (Rom. 1:25). However we prefer to express it, there is nothing more debasing than to dethrone the Lord Jesus in the area of our worship and service.

This condition leads to a desolation of heart. Think of it! A life with no enrichment in Christ, no refreshment in Christ, no contentment in Christ. Here is barrenness and uselessness personified. In this state of desolation we become candidates for God's judgment. Jesus said, "If anyone does not abide in Me, he is cast out as a branch and is withered; and they gather them and throw them into the fire, and they are burned" (John 15:6).

This was what had happened in the church of Corinth when certain of the believers were physically cut off by the verdict of God. The risen Saviour warned the church at Ephesus that unless the believers repented and returned to their first love, He would remove the candlestick out of its place (Rev. 2:5). We cannot tamper with God's conditions without facing His condemnation. We have seen areas of our country where once thousands of noble trees grew, but a careless camper permitted a fire to start that consumed acres and acres of these giants of the forest. So will one sin kindle the Lord's wrath against us so that our lives will be desolated and devastated.[7]

God's purpose of love is to lavish upon us the abounding provisions which He has made available in Christ. But His conditions are equally clear and demanding: He expects nothing less than total obedience. Only then can we go in and possess all that He has provided for us. Failure to do this leads to deceitfulness, disobedience, debasement, and desolation. Let us see to it that we do not find ourselves in the land that does not yield her fruit, but rather in the land that flows with milk and honey, grain and wine, oil and cattle. Living in such a land will mean nothing less than living in the place of blessing. Oh to heed, then, the words of the psalmist who said, "Trust in the Lord, and do good; dwell in the land, and feed on His faithfulness" (Ps. 37:3).

The most fulfilling and rewarding experience possible is to be found in going places with God.

# Footnotes

## Chapter 1

[1]A. Naismith, *A Treasury of Notes, Quotes, & Anecdotes for Sermon Building* (Grand Rapids: Baker), #178, p. 45.

[2]A. Naismith, *1200 Notes, Quotes, & Anecdotes* (London: Pickering & Ingles, Ltd.), #513, p. 90.

[3]*Ibid.,* #374, p. 66.

[4]Larry Poland, "Rise to Conquer," *Christian Herald* (1979), pp. 63-64.

[5]*Lowell's Poetical Works* (New York: Thomas Y. Crowell), p. 200.

[6]Aquilla Webb, *1,000 Evangelistic Illustrations* (New York: Harper & Brothers), pp. 103-104.

[7]Gladis and Gordon DePree, *A Blade of Grass* (Grand Rapids: Zondervan), p. 33.

[8]Aquilla Webb, *1,000 New Illustrations* (New York: Harper & Brothers), p. 99.

[9]Charles H. Stevens, *The Wilderness Journey* (Chicago: Moody Press), p. 101.

[10]Walter B. Knight, *3,000 Illustrations for Christian Service* (Grand Rapids: Eerdmans), p. 742.

[11]George Beverly Shea, "The Wonder of It All," Copyright 1956 by Chancel Music, Inc.

[12]James Mahoney, *Journey into Fullness* (Nashville: Broadman), p. 48.

## Chapter 2

[1]Quoted in *Dawnings,* ed. Phyllis Hobe (Waco, TX: Word Books). Copyright Guideposts Associates, Inc., Carmel, NY, p. 152.

[2]LeRoy Eims, *What Every Christian Should Know about Growing* (Wheaton: Victor Books), p 67.

[3]Phyllis Hobe, *Dawnings,* p. 207.

[4]Walter B. Knight, *Knight's Treasury of Illustrations* (Grand

Rapids: Eerdmans), p. 92.

[5]*Ibid.*, p. 148.

[6]Sam Shoemaker, *Extraordinary Living for Ordinary Men* (Grand Rapids: Zondervan), p. 25.

[7]G. B. F. Hallock, *2500 Best Modern Illustrations* (New York: Harper & Row), p. 289.

## Chapter 3

[1]A. Naismith, *1200 Notes, Quotes, and Anecdotes* (London: Pickering & Ingles, Ltd.), p. 89.

[2]Walter B. Knight, *Knight's Treasury of Illustrations* (Grand Rapids: Eerdmans), p. 304.

[3]Quoted by Major D. W. Whittle.

[4]W. E. Bierderwolf, *The Growing Christian* (Winona Lake, IN: The Winona Publishing Co.), pp. 11-12.

[5]F. Crossley Morgan as quoted by Walter B. Knight, *Knight's Master Book of New Illustrations* (Grand Rapids: Eerdmans), p. 45.

[6]Adapted from W. B. Knight in *Knight's Treasury of Illustrations* (Grand Rapids: Eerdmans).

## Chapter 4

[1]J. S. B. Monsell, *Hymns of Consecration and Faith* (London: Marshall, Morgan & Scott), p. 11.

[2]A. Naismith, *A Treasury of Notes, Quotes, & Anecdotes for Sermon Building* (Grand Rapids: Baker), p. 190.

[3]Quoted in *Dawnings*, ed. Phyllis Hobe (Waco, TX: Word Books). Copyright Guideposts Associates, Inc., Carmel, NY, p. 69.

[4]Walter B. Knight, *Knight's Illustrations for Today* (Chicago: Moody Press), p. 244.

[5]A. Naismith, *A Treasury of Notes, Quotes, & Anecdotes for Sermon Building* (Grand Rapids: Baker), p. 233.

[6]Helena Garrett, *A Threefold Cord* (London: Marshall, Morgan & Scott), p. 294.

[7]Brother Lawrence, *The Practice of the Presence of God* (Nashville: The Upper Room Publishing Co.), p. 32.

## Chapter 5

[1]G. H. C. MacGregor, *Into His Likeness* (Old Tappan, NJ: Revell), pp. 63-64.

[2]Charles L. Allen, "Freedom of the Will," *Hymns for the Family of God* (Nashville: Paragon Associates, Inc.), p. 599.

[3]Lloyd J. Oglivie, *Life Without Limits* (Waco, TX: Word Books), p. 178.

[4]Ted S. Rendall (used by permission).

[5]Walter Knight, *Knight's Illustrations for Today* (Chicago: Moody Press), p. 236.

[6]John Wesley as quoted in *Celebration of Discipline* by Richard J. Foster (New York: Harper & Row), p. 31.

[7]Paul E. Billheimer, *Destined for the Throne* (Fort Washington, PA: Christian Literature Crusade), p. 100.

[8]Arthur W. Pink, *Gleanings in Exodus* (Chicago: Moody Press), p. 144.

## Chapter 6

[1]F. W. Boreham as quoted in *1200 Notes, Quotes, & Anecdotes* by A. Naismith (London: Pickering & Ingles, Ltd.), pp. 35-36.

[2]W. Spencer Walton, *Redemption Songs* (London: Pickering & Ingles, Ltd.), p. 438.

[3]Adela Rogers St. Johns, *Tell No Man* (New York: Doubleday & Co., Inc.), pp. 100-101.

[4]Edward H. Bickersteth, "Peace, Perfect Peace," *Hymns for the Family of God* (Nashville: Paragon Associates, Inc.), p. 491.

[5]A. Naismith, *1200 Notes, Quotes, & Anecdotes* (London: Pickering & Ingles, Ltd.), p. 212.

[6]*Ibid.*, #216, p. 38.

[7]Gene A. Getz, *The Measure of a Man* (Glendale, CA: Regal Books), p. 178.

[8]*The Glory Christian* (London: Marshall Brothers), p. 57.

[9]Adapted by Ted S. Rendall (used by permission).

## Chapter 7

[1]Ted W. Engstrom, *What in the World Is God Doing?* (Waco, TX: Word Books).

[2]Quoted in *Dawnings*, ed. Phyllis Hobe (Waco, TX: Word Books). Copyright Guideposts Associates, Inc., Carmel, NY, p. 154.

[3]Walter B. Knight, *Knight's Treasury of Illustrations* (Grand Rapids: Eerdmans), p. 429.

[4]Walter B. Knight, *Knight's Master Book of New Illustrations* (Grand Rapids: Eerdmans), p. 730.

[5]Ted S. Rendall (used by permission).

[6]A. Naismith, *1200 Notes, Quotes, & Anecdotes* (London: Pickering & Ingles, Ltd.), p. 17.

[7]Walter B. Knight, *3,000 Illustrations for Christian Service* (Grand Rapids: Eerdmans), pp. 35-36.

[8]*Ibid.*, p. 31.

[9]Bryan Jeffery Leech, "A Pledge of Trust," *Hymns for the Family of God* (Nashville: Paragon Associates, Inc.), p. 74.

## Chapter 8

[1]Clarence Macartney, *Macartney's Illustrations* (New York: Abingdon), p. 302.

[2]A. Naismith, *A Treasury of Notes, Quotes, & Anecdotes for Sermon Building* (Grand Rapids: Baker), p. 46.

[3]A. Naismith, *1200 Notes, Quotes, & Anecdotes* (London: Pickering & Ingles, Ltd.), p. 48.

[4]Sam Shoemaker, *Extraordinary Living for Ordinary Men* (Grand Rapids: Zondervan), p. 15.

[5]Walter B. Knight, *Knight's Master Book of New Illustrations* (Grand Rapids: Eerdmans), p. 716.

[6]Walter B. Knight, *Up-to-the-Minute Illustrations* (Chicago: Moody Press), p. 57.

[7]Sam Shoemaker, pp. 35-36.

[8]Thomas O. Chisholm, "Living for Jesus," Copyright 1917 by

Heidelberg Press. Renewed 1945 (extended) by C. Harold Lowden. Assigned to the Rodeheaver Co. (Nashville: Paragon Associates, Inc.), p. 462.

## Chapter 9
[1]Pann Baltz, "A Certain Uncertain Future," *Hymns for the Family of God* (Nashville: Paragon Associates, Inc.), p. 111.

[2]John Caldwell Craig as quoted in *Sourcebook for Speakers* by E. Doan, (Grand Rapids: Zondervan).

[3]Walter B. Knight, *Knight's Master Book of New Illustrations* (Grand Rapids: Eerdmans), p. 527.

[4]Ted S. Rendell (used by permission).

[5]Rosalind Goforth, *Goforth of China* (Toronto: McClelland & Stewart, Ltd.), pp. 17-18.

[6]G. Franklin Allee, *Evangelistic Illustrations* (Chicago: Moody Press), p. 122.

[7]Harold P. Barker, *Windows in Words* (London: Pickering & Ingles, Ltd.), p. 116.

[8]Frances R. Havergal, *The Keswick Hymn Book* (London: Marshall, Morgan & Scott), distributed by Christian Literature Crusade.

## Chapter 10
[1]Adapted from *Evangelistic Illustrations* by G. F. Allee (Chicago: Moody Press), pp. 199-200.

[2]Walter B. Knight, *Knight's Master Book of New Illustrations* (Grand Rapids: Eerdmans), p. 28.

[3]*Ibid.*, pp. 477-478.

[4]Al Bryant, *1,000 New Illustrations* (Grand Rapids: Zondervan), p. 65.

[5]Ted S. Rendall (adapted, used by permission).

[6]Ted S. Rendall (used by permission).

[7]Ted S. Rendall (used by permission).

248.4
OL45

69910

LINCOLN CHRISTIAN COLLEGE